Excellence

Excellence

Every Classroom, Every Lesson, Every Day

Michael Horton

ROWMAN & LITTLEFIELD
Lanham • Boulder • New York • London

Published by Rowman & Littlefield
An imprint of The Rowman & Littlefield Publishing Group, Inc.
4501 Forbes Boulevard, Suite 200, Lanham, Maryland 20706
www.rowman.com

6 Tinworth Street, London SE11 5AL, United Kingdom

Copyright © 2020 by Michael Horton

All rights reserved. No part of this book may be reproduced in any form or by any electronic or mechanical means, including information storage and retrieval systems, without written permission from the publisher, except by a reviewer who may quote passages in a review.

British Library Cataloguing in Publication Information Available

Library of Congress Cataloging-in-Publication Data

Names: Horton, Michael, 1972- author.
Title: Excellence : every classroom, every lesson, every day / Michael Horton.
Description: Lanham, Maryland : Rowman & Littlefield, [2019] | Summary: "Join Dr. Esposito, the principal of a school with a reputation for eating administrators alive, on her journey to becoming a great educational leader and influencer. Dr. Esposito uses foundational leadership books to create a leadership philosophy centered around servant leadership to students while creating 360-degree leaders within the school"— Provided by publisher.
Identifiers: LCCN 2019042161 (print) | LCCN 2019042162 (ebook) |
  ISBN 9781475855463 (cloth) | ISBN 9781475855470 (paperback) |
  ISBN 9781475855487 (epub)
Subjects: LCSH: Educational leadership. | Education—Philosophy.
Classification: LCC LB2806 .H648 2019 (print) | LCC LB2806 (ebook) | DDC
  371.2—dc23
LC record available at https://lccn.loc.gov/2019042161
LC ebook record available at https://lccn.loc.gov/2019042162

I would like to dedicate this book to my wife Josie and my children Michael Jr. and Krystal. The time that I spent writing was time that was not spent with them. I appreciate the patience and understanding.
"Valuing time with your family does not mean you've
lost your ambition. Define success for yourself."
Claire Shipman

Contents

Preface		xi
Introduction		xiii
1	The Beginning of the End	1
	Leadership Reference: *Good to Great*	6
	Reflection Questions	6
2	Professor Scaffale	7
	Leadership Reference: *Good to Great* Part II	11
	Reflection Questions	12
3	Driving the Flywheel	13
	Leadership Reference: *Drive*	15
	Reflection Questions	15
4	Turned Inside Out	17
	Leadership Reference: *Drive* Part II and InsideOut Coaching	20
	Reflection Questions	21
5	The Way Forward	23
	Leadership Reference: *Tribes*	26
	Reflection Questions	27
6	Seeing through New Eyes	29
	Leadership Reference: *Visible Learning*	32
	Reflection Questions	32
7	Influence of Gold	33
	Leadership Reference: *The Art of Influence*	35
	Reflection Questions	35

8	The Breakthrough	37
	Leadership Reference: The Breakthrough Coach	39
	Reflection Questions	39
9	Taking a Walk	41
	Leadership Reference: *Instructional Rounds*	43
	Reflection Questions	44
10	Getting REAL	45
	Leadership Reference	47
	Reflection Questions	47
11	Flipping 360 Degrees	49
	Leadership Reference: *The 360 Degree Leader*	52
	Reflection Questions	52
12	A Simple Plan	53
	Leadership Reference: *Learning by Doing*	58
	Reflection Questions	58
13	Positive Deviance	59
	Leadership Reference: *Influencer*	62
	Reflection Questions	62
14	By Name and by Need	63
	Leadership Reference: *Mentoring 101*	66
	Reflection Questions	67
15	Bottom Up When Possible, Top Down When Necessary	69
	Leadership Reference: *How Did That Happen?* and *What Great Principals Do Differently*	72
	Reflection Questions	73
16	Perfect Practice	75
	Leadership Reference: *Practice Perfect*	76
	Reflection Questions	77
17	Thank You	79
	Leadership Reference: *Crucial Conversations*	81
	Reflection Questions	82
18	Vital Behaviors	83
	Leadership Reference: *How to Win Friends and Influence People*	86
	Reflection Questions	87
19	Love and Trust	89
	Leadership Reference: *The Speed of Trust*	91
	Reflection Questions	92

20	El Niño	93
	Leadership Reference: *Servant Leadership*	96
	Reflection Questions	96
21	The Surprise	97
	Leadership Reference: *The Motivation Breakthrough*	99
	Reflection Questions	100
22	You Raise Me Up	101
	Leadership Reference	102
	Reflection Questions	102
23	The Shallow Pool	103
	Leadership Reference	105
	Reflection Questions	105
24	The Matrix	107
	Leadership Reference: *Radical Candor*	111
	Reflection Questions	112
25	Epilogue and Discussion	113
Acknowledgments		125
About the Author		127

Preface

If your actions inspire others to dream more, learn more, do more, and become more, you are a leader.

—John Quincy Adams

I had been out of the classroom for three days before the first time that I had the question directed at me, "And how long have you been out of the classroom?" This question is normally used to justify ignoring the advice of a professional developer. Because of my unconventional path straight from the classroom to the county office, my role included coaching principals and district office administrators without having been one myself. To overcome this deficit and to avoid hearing this pointed question anymore, I read night and day everything that I could find on becoming a great leader and also observed, studied, and spoke at length with the great leaders around me.

I started a blog called *Motivational School Leadership* about my book studies and I shared summaries of books that I was reading with my colleagues. Those blogs and summaries were the spark that eventually led to this book. Since many of my favorite leadership authors write their books as fables (Lencioni, Rohn, Widener, Brewerton, Lundin, Johnson, etc.), I decided that I would also tell a realistic fictional story of how educational leaders can use these valuable resources to improve their practice.

The stories in this fable all have their genesis in real experiences. At two county offices, I visited more than a hundred schools and interacted with many dozens of leaders and teams of teachers. These interactions influenced my development as a leader and I hope that the stories will influence yours as well.

This book certainly does not contain references to every great leadership book that has ever been written. The books within are those that have affected my leadership philosophy the most. I hope that they will serve as examples of how leaders might use these and other leadership books to change their own leadership philosophies. These books may not resonate with you and that is perfectly acceptable, but the included examples will demonstrate how leadership books that do resonate with you can change how you lead your school.

In addition to these lessons, I hope that this fable also communicates another valuable message that I have learned over and over again in my career, relationships are everything. Without positive connections, leaders will be ineffective in influencing change. Without influence, a leader is inadequate. It is my belief that leadership skills can be learned. When combined with empathy and the soul of a servant leader to build strong relationships, influence will be deep and a community of educators will be formed for student success.

The book is structured in such a way as to blend current scenes from Carmen Esposito's retirement celebration and flashbacks throughout her career. These sections are separated by the following symbol: ❀.

Chapters that include a mention of a leadership book will have a section at the end (referred to as Leadership References), giving a short summary of the pertinent sections of the book. The summaries are not a replacement for reading the books in their entirety, but will hopefully be teasers to download some of the books that are of interest to you. There are also Reflection Questions at the end of each chapter to help you apply the lessons of the chapter to your own work.

You may follow the author on Twitter (@ExcellenceInEd3) to discuss some of the questions and ideas from the book with a professional network of educators. The author will also share resources on Twitter to accompany the book and to connect with the leadership books within.

Introduction

A mountain of research demonstrates, and basic logic confirms, how valuable teachers are to the success of a school. Doug Reeves is quoted as saying, "When it comes to student performance on reading and math tests, a teacher is estimated to have two to three times the impact of any other school factor, including services, facilities, and even leadership." This might suggest that school leaders are not very important.

When one considers that school leaders are charged with hiring, training, and retaining teachers, it becomes clear that a school leader's job is important in staffing a school full of amazing teachers. I believe that beyond hiring the best teachers, an administrator's job is to also do everything within their power to ensure that teachers have the autonomy to teach great lessons and that administrators move mountains to remove obstacles that interfere with this mission.

I worked at a county office, coaching principals, leadership teams, and departments, often at persistently underperforming schools during the No Child Left Behind (NCLB) era. I saw a lot of good come from the accountability measures that were part of NCLB at struggling schools, but the strict accountability also led to a counterproductive decrease in motivation and creativity among teachers and a spike in compliance-based activity.

During this phase in educational history, obstacles were being placed in front of creative, excellent, and well-meaning teachers. This was the opposite of what I believe that good administrators should do. At my current school, we ensure that there are no interruptions to classes. We do not even have an intercom system. We do not have assemblies during class time. We minimize useless paperwork. We buy our teachers office supplies and do not put limits on photocopies. We protect them from useless meetings. We try to do everything possible so that they can focus on connecting with students and creating engaging lessons.

I say this not to brag, but to encourage. As an administrator, it sometimes feels as if micromanagement is the only way to get things done. But I wish to shout from the rooftops that it is not. My current school was ranked by *U.S. News & World Report* as the best high school in the county and ninth in the state out of more than 2,500 high schools. We give our teachers as much autonomy as humanly possible.

As you will see in the coming pages, I did not come into administration with this philosophy and I did not learn it in my administrative credential classes. I came to this philosophy from reading everything that I could about leadership and by studying amazing leaders. Most of the seminal books in leadership are not written for educators, but for CEOs. I digested these books to pull out nuggets that apply to schools. I encourage you to do the same.

This book demonstrates the culmination of how I came to believe in this philosophy as well as summaries of many of the leadership and motivation books that changed the trajectory of my career. It is packaged in the fabled story of a respected principal flashing back through her career at all of the books and experiences that changed her life.

I hope that some of the books in the story will pique your interest and you will read through their pages to change your own trajectory as well as the trajectories of the teachers and students you work with. If the books here do not pique your interest, I hope dearly that they convince you that there are answers out there in leadership books and you will seek out books that do resonate with your own personal leadership philosophy.

The leadership concept that has changed my thinking the most is that of Daniel Pink. He posits that motivation is based upon three factors: autonomy, mastery, and purpose. I have built my leadership philosophy around these three ideas and have helped design a school around them as well. The only thing that I believe is missing from this list is the importance of relationships. If a follower truly feels a connection with you and knows that you care about them in return, they will go above and beyond the call of duty to serve students.

Please take this book and create your own list of trusted sources of leadership motivation whether audiobooks, podcasts, blogs, or your network on social media and use them to strive for *Excellence: Every Classroom, Every Lesson, Every Day.*

Chapter 1

The Beginning of the End

The growth and development of people is the highest calling of leadership.

—Harvey Firestone

The enormous board room was filled to capacity and everyone in attendance had tears in their eyes and smiles on their faces. Scanning the room, one could see that this clearly was not the typical meeting that takes place in this room. Seated at the front table were important looking people dressed in business attire with expensive shoes and fancy purses. They sat up straight and paid close attention.

The table to the right of that esteemed group hosted a gathering all dressed in Hawaiian shirts. Everyone sitting at the table to the left of the stage had clown noses on. There were costumes, crazy makeup, strange hats, and retro soccer uniforms throughout the standing-room-only board room and each one had a story behind it.

Most people thought that the history teachers were standing together in the back because all of the seats were full, but they had arrived early to ensure that these seats would be available. It was an inside joke that only a handful of people in the room understood. The giant clipboards and oversized red pens were part of the joke too.

One table of physical education teachers had helium balloons floating straight up from the buttons on the top of baseball caps. The superintendent, cabinet, and board members were at the well-dressed table near the front of the stage. The stage was set up with a podium and five metal folding chairs. The mayor made a surprise visit and more than two hundred seats were filled with teachers, counselors, instructional aides, custodians, office managers, and parents. Her impact reached far and wide.

On the well-adorned stage, the third chair from the left was empty as the retired superintendent, Dr. Vasquez, was at the podium with tears in her eyes too. She was comfortable in front of crowds and stood confidently at the podium with her tear-soaked handkerchief gripped tightly. She continued her story, "When I heard that Dr. Espo . . . sorry, Carmen (she looked at Carmen and winked, adding parenthetically that she hates to be called 'Dr. Esposito')."

Dr. Vasquez restarted, "When I heard that . . . Carmen . . . was retiring," she continued, "22 years of memories flashed through my mind from when I interviewed Carmen for the principal position, to when I pinned the state Principal of the Year award on her, from welcoming her back after defeating cancer, to watching her accept the Blue Ribbon Award and giving all of the credit to those around her."

"I've stood next to her in good times, celebrations, and awards and during bad times, tears, and legal battles. We've been soaking wet in the rain together and we've been covered in sweat in over 100 degree weather together. We've had paint in our hair together, and come to think of it, we've even been drenched in pineapple juice together, too. Through it all, she has remained positive, uplifting, and optimistic. I consider her my best friend. Many of us in this room consider Carmen our best friend. She looks out for us more than herself, she cares about us like her own family, and she would do anything to protect us. That's my definition of a best friend."

As everyone in attendance agreed with that statement, the room exploded with cheers and tears again. Dr. Vasquez was now so visibly emotional that she couldn't continue speaking any longer. She walked back to where Carmen was sitting, hugged her, and the two walked together toward the microphone on the fancy podium. "I present to you, the newly retired, and everyone's best friend . . . Dr. Carmen Esposito!" The room exploded in clapping, cheers, and smiles through tears and "What are we going to do now?" looks.

Carmen was very uncomfortable as the center of attention, so she was dying inside waiting for the applause to subside but the clamor only seemed to get louder and louder as time passed uncomfortably slowly. She was thrilled and embarrassed, honored and humbled all at once. She wanted to run, but knew that she would not get past the first row of tables before being dragged back on stage. So, she clenched her jaw, as she always does when she's nervous, and waited anxiously in front of hundreds of her friends, colleagues, and fans. Many of the same memories that had just coursed through Dr. Vasquez's mind were also coursing through Carmen's mind and she began to second-guess her decision to retire this year while she continued to wait for the applause to subside.

Carmen said into the microphone, "Thank you Dr. Vasquez," but nobody could hear her because the applause had still not subsided, in fact, it had grown even louder. She grinned a mischievous smile as a thought passed through her mind. She clapped her hands twice and like magic, the rumble in the room stopped and a gigantic pair of claps came back at her followed by hysterical laughter.

One of her first "non-negotiables" implemented schoolwide were "clock catchers" or strategies to save class time and contribute to increased instructional minutes. It would be a monumental understatement to say that this idea went over like a lead balloon initially.

Since, in hindsight, these non-negotiables have paid great dividends for an entire generation of students and are an integral part of the school's culture now, the faculty can finally laugh about their storied past. Hearing those claps thunder back at her made her feel accomplished and a little more comfortable on stage. A little more comfortable was still nowhere near comfortable, however her hands trembled a little less, and she felt like she might be able to speak without crying.

Carmen began once again, "There are so many wonderful people in this room who change the lives of students every single day. I don't deserve any of this; I should be throwing a thank-you party for all of you." This comment was met with the usual, "Come on!" and "You still aren't going to take any credit?" But that's just the type of leader that Carmen is.

Staring blankly at the wall in the back of the room where memory-inducing posters were hung, she dropped her note cards and said, "I want to tell you all a story that nobody in the room has heard, not even Dr. Vasquez, my best friend." The crowd giggled again since Dr. Esposito referred to everyone in the room as her "best friend."

"When I first interviewed for this principal position, it was because my husband had just lost his job and I had just been told that I was pregnant. We had no medical insurance and no income. I took a taxi to the interview because we had to sell my car to pay the rent. I had little motivation and no long-term goals. I interviewed for all of the wrong reasons and I knew the history of this school and the reputation that it had for eating administrators alive. I had applied at ten other schools and hadn't even gotten through the paper screening."

An understanding, empathetic wave of nods passed through the room. Those who had been around since the beginning remembered like it was last year. A great deal had changed since those early days in Carmen's tenure and the people in this room had witnessed the transformation and all of the hard work in the trenches that lead to its fruition.

"When the assistant principal was upset because he didn't get the principal job and transferred to Norman High, I was completely by myself and I have never felt so alone. I was surrounded by more than 100 teachers and 2,000 students and I felt completely alone. The first week, I broke up four fights, called 911 three times, got assaulted by a parent, was spat on by a student, had two campus supervisors quit, and had my car vandalized . . . twice. The district office reminded me several times that this was the lowest performing school in the district and if I could just last a year or two, I could request a transfer to a 'more successful' school."

Carmen paused briefly and then continued, "The school was crumbling around me and like I always do, I placed all of the blame on my own shoulders." The whole crowd agreed because self-blame was definitely Carmen's modus operandi. She lived the motto "take blame, give credit" to an extreme. Whenever she was praised, she would immediately list all of the people who deserved the credit besides her. It was one of Jim Collins' characteristics of a Level 5 leader, but it is very difficult on the leader of a struggling organization.

"To compensate for my perceived failures, I buried myself in my work 6 days a week, 18 hours a day. I put on weight, my blood pressure was through the roof, and I started smoking again. By the end of that first year, I'd had a miscarriage, met weekly with a therapist, and found myself speaking with my husband's divorce lawyers. She, the lawyer, had to come to the school to meet with me because I was too busy to make the trip three quarters of a mile to her office."

The tone of the room had now changed because only Carmen's new husband of twelve years knew any of these stories. All of the people in the room who worked there that first year knew that she struggled but had no idea the depth of her struggles. Like they would learn over Carmen's first few years, this is how she deals with stress. She locks it up deep inside and buries herself in her work while blaming herself for any failures.

Carmen continued speaking to a silent crowd hanging on her every word. "Before Alan left me, we had one deep conversation that ended with him saying to me, 'What are you about? What's important to you? You've lost your direction.' I was devastated. Never in my life had anyone been so insulting to me . . . neither had anyone ever been so accurate in their assessment of me. When I didn't show up to school for a few days after that, rumors began circulating that I had abandoned ship just like the last four or five principals before me. People actually started to take items off of my desk to decorate their own desks, assuming that I wasn't even coming back to pick up my personal belongings."

In response, a voice from the center of the room called out, "Sorry about that Carmen! I still have that candle on my desk and you still can't have it back!" It came from the health teacher at the time, now the athletic director at another school, and even though the audience was on the edge of their seats in surprise and anticipation, laughter still advanced through the room.

"But that question, 'What are you about?' is what I was contemplating, what I was obsessing over, and what would eventually change my life. I spent several days and nights without any sleep, contemplating what I am about and what's important to me. I had big ideas, small ideas, grand ideas, and terrible ideas, but in the end, I rejected them all. I called my mother and my grandmother, signed up for Yoga, and even considered going vegan to try to get the ideas flowing." That comment generated laughter as it was well known that Carmen preferred doughnuts over any other food on the planet.

"After beating myself up for days, what finally brought me back to Earth was thinking about some of the students whose lives I had literally changed for the better as a teacher. I set up lunch with the mother of one former student who I had impacted greatly. I remembered one afternoon when I popped open a can of diet soda in class and he flipped around quickly. When I asked why he reacted that way, he responded, 'At my house, that sound means one hour until the beatings start.' I ended up calling CPS and helping his family find a shelter and counseling. His mother and I became very close."

"We discussed the past and the future of their marriage, her family, the economics of being a single mother, and her son's education. She shared stories that made me wonder how her son ever made it to school after one of his father's blowouts. The turning point was at this lunch meeting when his mom looked me straight in the eyes and asked me, 'What are you about?' I couldn't remember for sure, but I think that she even used the exact same words as Alan."

Carmen did not know exactly where she was going with this story, but she continued, "I finally decided that I was about changing the lives of students who had nobody on their sides, not their parents, not their counselors, and I hate to say it—but at the time—not their administrators or teachers either." It was easy to see all of the white-haired heads nodding in agreement with vague memories of how things used to be. "I knew that in the history of education, every great school has been filled with great teachers. So, in addition to becoming a great administrator, I knew that I also had to figure out a way to inspire and motivate a school full of great teachers."

There was movement in the room, but not much, maybe some breathing sounds but nothing else. It was perfectly silent as Carmen told her stories of struggles and perseverance. As Carmen glanced around the room, she made eye contact with dozens of friends, colleagues, followers, and leaders. She could tell detailed stories about the lives of each person in the room, their families, and their goals and dreams.

Carmen felt satisfied with her accomplishments and proud of the success she had helped ignite in others. She felt guilty about retiring and leaving them all behind, but her health, both emotional and physical, prevented her from continuing any longer. Both the district office and the county office had offered her consulting jobs. She did not decline the options completely but also had very little interest or energy left to continue working.

LEADERSHIP REFERENCE: *GOOD TO GREAT*

Carmen refers to Level 5 leadership in Jim Collins' *Good to Great: Why Some Companies Make the Leap and Others Don't*. In this blueprint for how to lead a good organization to greatness, Collins describes what the epitome of great leadership, Level 5 leadership, would look like. The two key characteristics unique to a Level 5 leader are humility and a ferocious will to affect something bigger than oneself.

Jim Collins described the levels of leadership as follows with each level containing the characteristics of the level below.

Level 1: Highly Capable Individual
Highly capable individuals do good work that contributes to the organization's mission mixed in with good work ethic, foundational knowledge, and requisite skills.

Level 2: Contributing Team Member
Contributing team members use their knowledge and skills to help their team accomplish bigger goals. Not only does a Level 2 leader work hard, but they work well with others also.

Level 3: Competent Manager
Competent managers have the skills of a contributing team member plus the project management and people management skills to lead the completion of tasks.

Level 4: Effective Leader
Effective leaders can motivate and inspire a team to work well together to achieve a common mission and vision. Many leaders peak out at this level and are considered successful leaders.

Level 5: Great Leader
Great leaders are not necessarily charismatic, but humble and highly driven. They have a strong ability to motivate others to passionately pursue a mission. People gladly and willingly follow these leaders and put more effort into their work than they are even asked to put in.

REFLECTION QUESTIONS

1. What are you about? What is it about educational leadership that gets you up every morning?
2. What would you like people to remember about you at your retirement party? Who would you like to be there?
3. What legacy would you like to leave in your current situation?

Chapter 2

Professor Scaffale

> *Greatness is not a function of circumstance. Greatness, it turns out, is largely a matter of conscious choice, and discipline.*
>
> —Jim Collins

The large room, decorated with memorabilia from a long career, was still silent as Carmen continued speaking. "I'd only been an assistant principal for three years and a principal for one year before my interview. I had taken a few years off from full-time work to raise Jonathan and he was now attending pre-school full time. I hadn't even set foot on a school campus since my last admin job 3 years ago when I applied for this job."

"It was clear that I didn't have the skills or the knowledge to make this turnaround happen, but my heart seemed ready. I truly believed that heart is the most important part of leadership, but I would go through phases where I began to doubt that. I had never worked with this particular demographic of students before, but I grew up in a similar area so overall, I felt like I might have the potential to be a decent leader." A lot of eyes rolled at that comments since most people in the room respected her current leadership skills a great deal.

Carmen was just telling a story now and did not really have a destination in mind or an overall point yet, but she was sure that eventually, she would figure it out. Although she always thought of herself as a pessimist, anyone else who described her always used positive terms. She never understood this paradox but she was happy about it. Carmen thought that she should now try to be more optimistic.

"Education journals touted research about turnaround schools and led with titles like, 'We Know How to Turn Schools Around. Why Aren't We Doing It?' But the articles were full of generalities and theoretical, state and federal policy-based solutions or pleas for more money for schools and higher pay for teachers. Of course this was at the same time that the economy was crashing and enrollment was declining because students were transferring to surrounding schools. Charter schools were beginning to flourish and many parents saw them as a viable alternative to the big, faceless comprehensive schools." This was a dark time in the school's history and Carmen realized that she was doing a terrible job getting more optimistic.

"With the decline in funding, I wasn't getting an assistant principal any time soon and that's when I started collaborating with Professor Scaffale, my only real friend at the time." At this, Dr. Esposito's mind began conjuring memories of that second year.

When Dr. Scaffale came into her life, Carmen was still going by "Mrs. Johnston" since she hadn't finished her doctorate yet and she was separated, but not yet divorced. After she returned from her soul-searching "leave of absence" as she liked to call it, the teachers were pleasantly surprised that she came back, but still not confident in her longevity. They figured that she would end up at the bottom of a long list of failed administrators that the school had seen in the last five years. There were two types of administrators at this school, the type that could not handle it and went to an "easier school" and those who used it as a stepping stone to higher position somewhere else, usually the district office.

Carmen still wasn't close to anyone at the school and she did not have a single teacher on the staff who she would consider her ally. She mostly sat in her office performing managerial duties, making sure that buses were on schedule, paychecks were signed, bills were paid, referees were on time to football games, and misbehavior was punished. She was miserable, teachers were miserable, and students were very miserable.

One afternoon, not long after Carmen returned to work, a history teacher stomped into the office and said to her, "Mrs. Johnston, the Social Studies department has decided that we will no longer attend your useless faculty meetings. They're a waste of our time and we could spend that time grading papers. So, none of us in the department will be at tomorrow's meeting and if you try to force us, we will file a grievance with my uncle in Human Resources." The department chair then spun around defiantly and marched out of the office with an air of victory.

Many moments later, Carmen realized that her mouth was still open and she had not moved for what felt like an hour since the teacher walked out. She closed her mouth and then shut the door to soak up what had just happened. Her professors had never covered any of this (as well as many other important things) in any of her educational administration master's degree classes. In fact, at one of the orientations, they actually stated that people interested in becoming site administrators should attend a different university because this program was about producing future professors of educational administration.

Carmen felt like future professors should be previously successful administrators and she did not understand the difference. She was under the impression that the training of future administrators and future professors of administration should be the same. As a result of this conversation, she did attend a different university, but the situation there was not much more helpful either.

By the end, she knew the names of all of the senate bills defining how schools are funded and the names of key historical court cases related to education, but didn't know how to motivate a teacher, run a faculty meeting, or how to give effective feedback during a classroom walkthrough. She had a lot of on-the-job learning to do and she hoped that Professor Scaffale would be her savior. But first things first, she had a social studies department to deal with immediately.

Carmen's first thought was to see what the teacher contract had to say about faculty meetings. She was not impressed by the contract which looked like it had not been updated in many years and was very district friendly. It was the smallest contract she had ever seen. According to the contract, teachers were required to attend "one 60-minute faculty meeting per month after school plus an additional 60 minutes per month during accreditation years. Unit members may not be required to meet before school, during their duty-free lunch, or during preparatory periods."

She won! She leaned back in her chair fingers locked behind her neck in a victorious pose. She was brought back to reality when her chair creaked and almost fell backward. She should have seen it as an omen. Immediately, she crafted an email,

> Teachers,
> Tomorrow is the second Wednesday of the month and this is a reminder that we'll be meeting as a faculty in the multi-purpose room from 2:45-3:40. According to your contract, all teachers may be required to attend one 60-minute meeting per month, so I will see you all tomorrow. Please bring the results of the last benchmark test with you so we can discuss it.
>
> Mrs. Johnston

It was perfect! She had butterflies in her stomach the entire day in anticipation of the reaction that she would receive. The teachers had no choice; they were required to attend the meeting. Something else had been eating at her since the strange interaction with the department chair. The social studies teachers had called her faculty meetings useless. That hurt deep down inside. Thinking back, she had tried to make the meetings happy, positive, and celebratory, and she filled them with fun, educational activities like she learned at a conference with icebreakers, team-building, and visioning activities.

This meeting, she was going to try to make extra special. Dr. Sandee from the district office owed her a favor, so with a single phone call, a guest speaker was scheduled to come and talk about the school's data. This would make the teachers sit up and listen for sure! She also spent the whole day planning every minute of the meeting from beginning to end so that there would be no time for mutiny. There is no way that anyone would ever call her faculty meetings useless again!

Carmen was so nervous that she stayed in her office until the last possible minute before leaving to the multipurpose room. She flung the office door open and walked out of the building when she was overcome by the feeling that she was going to lose her lunch. She thought to herself, "I didn't even eat lunch, so I'm ok." She was able to calm herself down a little and tiptoe hesitantly to the meeting.

Carmen walked through the doors to see 100 chairs in the middle of the floor almost completely filled and she breathed a sigh of relief; a weight lifted off of her shoulders. Then out of the corner of her eye, she noticed the social studies department crowded around a table in the back of the room. These history teachers had stacks of papers in clipboards and red pens set up and ready to grade papers during the meeting.

"Noooooo!" she thought, "I lost! They won!"

Her pace quickened, as did her pulse, as she walked over to handle this situation with authority. Before she got half way there, the department chair stood up and said, "Mrs. Johnston, the contract might allow you to force us to come to these meetings, but you cannot make us participate. We have papers to grade and we will NOT participate in your useless meetings anymore." He slammed himself back down in the chair and took up his red pen again. His colleagues followed suit.

She was furious! But, he was correct. After all of the mistakes she had made leading up to this moment, Carmen knew that trying to force them to participate would be the worst mistake of them all at this point. She wanted to cry and shrink back into her depressed shell but had nearly a hundred teachers waiting patiently for her meeting to begin.

In her introductory comments, Carmen explained that one of her favorite authors, Jim Collins, explained that an organization cannot grow unless they face brutal facts first. She explained that along those lines, Dr. Sandee from the district office was going to share some benchmark test data with them. In hindsight, she had set Dr. Sandee up for failure from the start.

Dr. Sandee arrived with flash drive in hand and a brilliant set of charts showing the teachers what terrible results the students were achieving and how all of the schools in the district were outperforming them. To Carmen's surprise, the teachers did not sit up in their chairs and listen intently. They did not take notes or ask for copies of the PowerPoint. They did not nod in agreement, not even a single one of them.

The teachers whispered to each other in disgust and asked pointed questions like, "Who wrote these tests? Have the questions been checked for validity and reliability? Were the 'bad questions' from last year removed before it was printed again this year? Have the people who wrote these tests ever seen the standards? Did you have a single teacher on the committee who wrote these questions?" Dr. Sandee was speechless and Mrs. Johnston was embarrassed. The social studies teachers were right, her faculty meetings ARE useless!

Before leaving, Dr. Sandee made the ultimate external presenter mistake and said something positive about the rival high school in the district. Visions of football games and wrestling matches went through the teachers' minds and the audience was officially lost and fuming inside even more than before. This faculty meeting was a disaster.

Comments like, "Who does she think she's talking to?" and "Did she really just go there? Doesn't she know that we are the stepchild in the district?" were thrown around. Carmen did not even close the meeting; she just sat depressed as the teachers slowly filed out sharing stories about how the evil Norman High School gets everything they want, including all of the good students. Since many of the teachers had been led to believe that the only way to improve a school is to attract better students, they had no motivation to improve because it was not their fault, in their minds, that students were struggling. If they could just attract better students and if the middle schools would just do a better job, everything would be better.

Dr. Sandee had never seen such resistance to one of her presentations before and sat staring at the charts to see if she had made a mistake somewhere. Her only mistake, it turns out, was accepting Carmen's invitation in the first place.

LEADERSHIP REFERENCE: *GOOD TO GREAT* PART II

Carmen referred once again to Jim Collins' *Good to Great*. In the book, Collins sets down a strong case that good is the enemy of great. Good organizations and good leaders become apathetic and as a result, never become great. Good gets accolades and wins awards, but great changes lives.

One of the caveats of becoming a great organization is facing brutal facts while never wavering from the mission. Since this pronouncement, entire books have been written about brutal honesty in leadership. Collins referred to this breakthrough in good to great companies as "The Stockdale Paradox."

James Stockdale was a Vietnam-era prisoner of war for eight years. He was tortured during that time and had no reason to believe he would ever get out. He surmised that the difference between himself and his more optimistic prison mates who did not survive was that he faced the brutal facts of his situation while they constantly held unrealistically positive expectations for the future. For educational leaders, positivity is a great trait, but not when it ignores brutal facts.

REFLECTION QUESTIONS

1. What do you believe are the attributes that make for an excellent educational leader?
2. Who is your mentor? Who do you model your leadership style after?
3. What brutal facts has your organization been avoiding? Are you ready to face them or is there some work to do first?

Chapter 3

Driving the Flywheel

Great vision without great people is irrelevant.

—Jim Collins

Carmen, still quivering at the microphone in front of a silent crowd, was now wondering if it was really a good idea to even tell this story. She had gone down a negative, personal road, but she was too far along now so she just continued. "Looking back at that time, I'm embarrassed how little I actually knew about leadership. In our administration classes, we read textbooks and posted on forums, but the learning was theoretical and the curriculum was written way high up in the 'Ivory Tower.'"

"They didn't teach me how important relationships are, how stressful the job can be, and how critical self-care is. And they certainly did not teach me how to apologize when I am wrong. And boy was I wrong a lot that first year! I knew nothing about being a leader and it was obvious to everyone around me. I had no idea what tomorrow would hold for me, but I kept thinking to myself, 'I have good intentions and I want to be a good leader, so I'll keep plugging away and things will get better.' Things weren't getting any better."

The audience did not want to laugh because they had grown to love her, but she was correct about being wrong so much and nothing was going well those first couple of years. A low rumble of laughs from brave souls and understanding glances from caring colleagues diffused through the room like a foul smell in a car with the windows closed. At this point in her career, Carmen's mantra was, "I may not know what I'm doing yet, but my heart is always in the right place."

Chapter 3

Carmen was dejected when she met with Professor Scaffale that week. They had so much to talk about but she had to settle her nerves and figure out where to begin. She told the professor the entire story of the faculty meeting without skipping a single depressing detail. There were tears galore and the trash can quickly filled with moist tissues.

"I don't think I can do this anymore," she confessed with her posture and facial expression screaming defeat. "Maybe I should just call it quits like all of the others. Why did I think I could do this when so many principals before me had failed? I'm like one of those pizza places that takes over a store front when another pizza place has just gone out of business there. What was I thinking?"

Professor Scaffale consoled and reassured her and then said to Carmen, "Sounds like there were three main parts of the meeting: Ice Breaker, Data Presentation, and Celebration. Why did you select those three things in particular?" Sheepishly, she replied, "Because that's what the teachers need. Jim Collins said that organizations cannot be truly great until they can face the brutal facts."

"Great, you've read Collins' *Good to Great*. That'll be a great foundation for our conversation today. Let's consider the flywheel concept. On your first day, how fast would you say the flywheel was turning?"

"I'd say that we didn't even have a flywheel yet." she said with a hint of pessimistic exaggeration, but not much.

The professor continued, "How fast do you think the flywheel should be turning before you start throwing brutal facts at it?" No response. "Would you consider the school to be a good school?" More tissues came out and her nearly inaudible response leaked from her lips, "No, not yet. Maybe it was too soon for brutal facts?"

"So, let's go back a step," the professor said supportively, "How many teachers did you speak to before you concluded that this meeting is exactly what they needed?"

"None, I just kn . . . Oh." Carmen paused for several deep breaths and then in desperation asked, "So, what should I have done instead?"

"Sounds like a simple question, doesn't it?" A small grin appeared on only one half of his mouth and one eyebrow raised. "Leadership is never that simple. How about this? I'm going to give you a copy of my absolute favorite leadership book and I think it might have some answers for you." He handed her a red and white book with the word "Drive" scrawled across the front.

"Hmm . . . Daniel Pink?" The book wasn't very thick and didn't look like any of the books she slogged through in college, so she questioned with a hint of skepticism, "This has some answers in it, huh? I'm willing to try anything." Carmen was skeptical, but she was really willing to try anything at this point.

They agreed to meet again in a week and discuss the book through the lens of improving faculty meetings. That would give them about two weeks to plan the next meeting. They both agreed that a school cannot become great without great teachers, great professional development, and great collaboration. Carmen was not the kind of person to wait a week to complete a task. She consumed the book in one evening and left Professor Scaffale a voicemail the very next day. The voicemail had a hint of hope in it.

LEADERSHIP REFERENCE: *DRIVE*

The "Flywheel" concept in Collins' *Good to Great* is referring to the consistent, intense effort over a long period of time that it would take to get a giant flywheel spinning and to keep it that way. Such it is with organizations also. Getting a mission and vision moving takes a similar intensely focused, long-term team effort of everyone moving in the same direction. The metaphor is apt to turnaround schools as well. One cannot turn a giant flywheel alone and even the best teams cannot get a flywheel spinning at top speed right away.

Daniel Pink's *Drive: The Surprising Truth about What Motivates Us* discusses new ideas in human motivation and will be discussed more after chapter 4. He contrasts the new ideas with "Motivation 1.0" where leaders simply met their followers' basic biological needs and "Motivation 2.0" or the "Carrot and Stick" model of motivation. Motivation 2.0 works for mundane tasks that do not require any creativity like getting teachers to turn in their grades on time.

However, "Carrot and Stick" motivation does not work for long-term, larger, less defined, and more creative endeavors like bringing an entire school up to reading at grade level. Pink describes his new proposal for motivation being appropriate for things like putting in the great effort to be a spectacular teacher.

REFLECTION QUESTIONS

1. When was the last time you felt like calling it quits? What caused it? How did you get over that feeling?
2. How do you plan your faculty meetings? How much input do teachers have?
3. How fast is your proverbial flywheel turning? What would it take to get it up to the speed that you dream about?

Chapter 4

Turned Inside Out

> *Leadership is about empathy. It is about having the ability to relate to and to connect with people for the purpose of inspiring and empowering their lives.*
>
> —Daniel Pink

Dr. Esposito still had tightness in her chest on stage because she hates being the center of attention and right now, she was the center of a room full of people on the edge of their seats. She was visualizing her original office, picturing the red and white book, and shaking a little as she continued with the story.

"I wasn't particularly happy with Professor Scaffale at that point. It was like he let me see deep inside myself and I really didn't like what I saw. I was already taking antidepressants and seeing a therapist so clearly this new self-disappointment wasn't going to help make the situation any better. I wanted to be great, I faced the brutal facts, I was pushing on the flywheel, but things were not getting any better. If something didn't change soon, I was finished professionally, personally, and physically," she said to a crowd that hadn't made a sound, maybe not even breathed, in several minutes.

"I was in a very dark place and things weren't getting any better. Professor Scaffale and Daniel Pink gave me a slight glimmer of hope, but it was going to take a lot more than better faculty meetings to turn this ship around. There was no light at the end of my very dark tunnel, hell there was no light and there was no tunnel."

After hearing the enthusiasm and excitement in her voicemail, Professor Scaffale agreed to meet sooner than the originally agreed-upon time. He was inspired by how quickly Carmen had finished the book. Upon entering the usually tidy office, he noticed an entire legal pad in the trash and crumpled paper strewn in a circle around the trash can and inquired, "Wow, what happened here? A binder exploded?"

Carmen laughed at herself and responded, "That was the plan I wrote yesterday for forcing the history teachers to believe that my staff meetings are amazing. There is the plan that I wrote for how to analyze test data. It was terrible. Here's the plan that I began for redesigning department meetings. There's no way the social studies teachers would have ever followed it. This book made me realize that all of these plans are horrible and doomed to failure."

"I see. Apparently Daniel Pink influenced you?" He added air quotes around the word "influenced" with a grin showing that he was proud of his clever wordplay since the book centered around motivation and influence.

She confessed, "My faculty meetings lacked autonomy, mastery, AND purpose! I think he wrote that book especially for me. But as you can see, I'm struggling to use it to fix my useless meetings." She added air quotes around "useless" to mock him a little and to show that she still had not gotten over the shock of her faculty meetings being called, and probably accurately called, useless.

"I know that *autonomy* is giving teachers some say in what we do in meetings and some freedom as to how we accomplish those things. *Mastery* is about sticking with one very important thing and practicing it until it's a part of our culture. I know that this school has a history of 'initiative fatigue' where they were presented one new program after another and never mastered any of them. And *purpose* is putting my quest to change students' lives at the forefront of every decision that I make, every dollar that I budget, and every minute that I spend with teachers."

The professor thought for a moment and asked, "What's your goal for these meetings?"

"Good question. I think that my goals are to bring faculty together, I want to bring them together like a family . . . a functional family, not a family like my own. Also, I want to help the teachers become stronger instructors in the classroom and I want them to connect with students better."

"Where would you say you are on a scale of 0 to 100 on each of those things?"

"I'd say that I'm at about 3 out of 100 on the family part and 25 out of 100 at helping them become better teachers. I'd say that they're already at about 70 out of 100 at being great teachers but with a large variation between the best and the worst. And there is very little culture of sharing best practices, so if something doesn't change, the standard deviation will remain high with huge variation from classroom to classroom."

"Wow! What have you already tried to do in order to improve those brilliant scores?" he joked to ease the pain of pointing out the painfully obvious.

"I give 'Teacher of the Month' awards at every meeting, I have them sit together in departments, we do friendly competitions, and once a week I bring doughnuts." At that moment, an English teacher, Mrs. Toms popped her head in and said, "Oh, I see you're busy, I'll come back later." Carmen wasn't sure if Mrs. Toms actually liked her or was being friendly because she had applied for the assistant principal position that had finally been advertised by human resources.

The district office had noticed Carmen's struggles—everybody within 50 miles had—so they agreed to try to find a way to hire an assistant principal. Carmen was terrified that they had noticed her struggles, but hopeful that she might get some help. After a few days of the position being advertised on the HR website, they took the post down and told her that they could not figure out a way to make the budget work out. Apparently, nobody had told Mrs. Toms yet.

Mrs. Toms would end up being Carmen's true best friend, the best assistant principal she ever had, and eventually a wonderful principal at Norman, the rival high school in the district. It was one of the greatest accomplishments of her career to help catalyze a highly effective leader and she felt a sense of pride in having helped her grow into the leader that she had become. She was similar enough to Carmen, but also added her own leadership style to her mission to move her very good school into the great category. It was a different mission than Carmen's, but required the same leadership skills.

Professor Scaffale glanced over his shoulder at Mrs. Toms and then continued after her speedy and mysterious exit, "So your scores are low and you've tried some motivation strategies like teacher of the month. After reading Drive, what additional ideas have you considered to increase motivation and the value of your faculty meetings?"

"I guess that I could send out a survey and ask what topics they'd like to cover. That would contribute some 'autonomy' to the meetings. But only a little. I could put some teachers in charge of planning the meetings. I've heard of these things called 'un-conferences' where I just set up meeting rooms and they congregate, determine the topic to discuss, and have a deep, free-flowing conversation about it. I could give them sticky dots and have them vote with colored dots which topics they'd like to cover in the future. I think that all of these are possible options."

She was feeling better as her mind started to focus on possibilities and solutions instead of dwelling on past failures. After a pause, Professor Scaffale asked, "Considering where you are, where you'd like to be, and the resources you have available to you, which one of those options seems reasonable in this specific situation?"

"I don't think that enough people would respond to the survey to make it worthwhile. I've never had very good luck getting people to respond to surveys. I'm not sure that we're ready for an un-conference quite yet. That's probably too big of a step. The colored dots still lack full autonomy since I'd be the one coming up with the list. So, I guess I could put some trusted teachers in charge of helping out with planning."

"Sounds like a good start. May I offer a suggestion?" After a vigorous nod from Carmen in the affirmative, he continued, "My suggestion comes in the form of another book. I don't carry this one in my laptop bag like I do with Daniel Pink, but I hope you'll pick up a copy of this book and we can discuss it again in a week and you'll still have more than two weeks to plan your next meeting." He scratched on a sticky note, "Tribes by Seth Godin."

"Before I go," he added, "I wanted to explain this process that we've just been through. I modeled for you a scaled down version of a process called 'InsideOut Coaching' that I highly recommend you consider using in your coaching interactions with teachers. It involves a process where you go through a GROW conversation and you ask: 'What are your Goals?,' 'What is your Reality?,' 'What are your Options?,' and 'What is your Way forward?' We'll do that last step next time after you read 'Tribes.' I'd recommend that you go through the full Inside Out Coaching training and you can have these coaching conversations with your teachers, too. It really puts most of the conversation in their hands and you simply have to ask the four questions, listen, and offer guidance if they ask for it."

Of course, Carmen wasn't one for theory, so she was scribbling notes about GROW on her tablet knowing that it would come in handy someday in the near future. She also put a note on her calendar to find a training to attend. She told her secretary she was headed out of the office for a while. When asked where she was headed, Carmen replied, "I'll be at the bookstore, but can you invent a better story than that for when teachers ask where I am? Otherwise, they'll think that I quit again and they'll start taking things off of my desk." She winked at the secretary, but honestly was only half joking about the cover story.

LEADERSHIP REFERENCE: *DRIVE* PART II AND INSIDEOUT COACHING

Daniel Pink's proposition of "Motivation 2.0" is featured in this chapter. The alternative to the carrot-and-stick method, Motivation 2.0 boils down to autonomy, mastery, and purpose. As described briefly in the chapter, human beings are motivated by:

(1) The autonomy to have control over the work that they do and how they do their jobs.
(2) Being given the time, tools, and support to fully master the knowledge and skills necessary to meet the organization's vision.
(3) Working on projects with a purpose beyond the mundane, being reminded of the purpose of their work, and being given the autonomy and ample time to master the skills to accomplish the tasks.

A mix of these three things, autonomy, mastery, and purpose, with a large dose of strong relationships is what builds high achieving teams and organizations. A school club, classroom, grade level, entire school, school district, county office, or state office could be built around these principles. Although these principles are very bottom up and grassroots, the freedom to pursue them, culture to not revert back to the status quo, and the resources to make them happen must come from the top.

InsideOut Development™ provides workshops and train-the-trainer sessions to learn more about the GROW model of InsideOut Coaching. An online search can reveal dates and locations for these workshops. The author has been trained in many different employee coaching and cognitive coaching models and this one has been the simplest to implement. The codevelopers of the GROW model itself, John Whitmore, Graham Alexander, and Alan Fine, have all written about how the method works as well and their work can be found online. Others have written books about the GROW model as part of a coaching program.

REFLECTION QUESTIONS

1. Every leader gets sad and frustrated, some even depressed. How do you cope with these feelings?
2. How do you provide autonomy for your teachers? How do you avoid initiative fatigue and give them time to master the important aspects of teaching?
3. What is your organization's purpose? How does it drive your organization? How is that communicated to your peers?

Chapter 5

The Way Forward

You can't have a tribe without a leader—and you can't be a leader without a tribe.

—Seth Godin

Carmen looked down at the table where Mrs. Toms was beaming up at her and there was a toy redwood tree at the center of the table, the kind you'd see on a toy train set, and around the base, it said, "Tribe Leaders." This table was full of people she had spent many hundreds of hours discussing, debating, loving, resenting, supporting, forgiving, and in the end, owing much of her success. Although it was part of her schtick to call everyone her best friend, she had a lot of true best friends at this table. Many of these friendships were forged as a result of this conversation with Professor Scaffale and this was one of the first turning points in her career.

Carmen continued, "Raise your hand if I've ever called you my best friend." Nearly every hand . . . no, every hand in the room went up. "There is an online dictionary that Mrs. Toms and I have spent far too much time looking up slang phrases that students have called each other and the definition entry for best friend says 'Best Friends are very special people in your life. They are the first people you think about when you make plans. They are the first people you go to when you need someone to talk to.' Based upon that definition, you all truly are my best friends."

"But this group sitting around that redwood tree there," she smiled and pointed down at the front table, "You all are beyond friends to me. Everything that this school has accomplished was in your hands. It took me time to learn to step back and just get out of your way, but it was the best decision I ever made. Who would have ever thought that the best leadership lesson I'd ever learn is to put great people in leadership positions and let them be great? Your passion is contagious—and so was the flu, remember that, Phil?" Phil, sitting at that front table, held the back of his hand to his forehead as if he had a fever.

"I originally intended for you all to spread my message to the masses, but you amplified my message, improved my message, and eventually, created your own much better message. It was probably the greatest thing I have done in my career and I didn't even do it intentionally at first."

When Professor Scaffale came back less than a week later, he could see a little more confidence in her face and he was also surprised to see four teachers sitting in her office. They all shook hands before departing and appeared to be friendly. That was a good sign—a great sign.

"What was that all about?" He asked, after the teachers exited the office.

She responded with a nervous smile, "Sorry, I couldn't wait for our conversation to begin implementing the 'Way Forward' that you hinted at last time. After reading Tribes, it was obvious what I had to do. I needed to identify some tribe leaders who are on board with the mission and start spreading the message. Godin says that tribes can be built around each other, a leader, or an idea. I want them to gather around the idea that all of our students can be successful if the school holds adults to high expectations and gives them enormous support."

"Exactly!" He responded and gave her a supportive squeeze on the shoulder as they sat down. "So, who were the teachers? Were they your department chairs?"

"No, not all department chairs," she responded, "because those are assigned by seniority alone according to the contract." She rolled her eyes and continued, "Seth Godin said that tribe leaders should be passionate, positive, influential, innovative people with leadership skills. Not all of my department chairs fit that bill. Remember Mrs. Toms who popped her head in last time?"

"I think she's going to be the leader of the tribe leaders. She is really stepping forward, has excellent ideas, and really believes in the mission. I'm excited! Maybe I CAN do this." Carmen was so excited that she vacillated between shaking Dr. Scaffale's hand, standing up to hug him, giving him a high five that it looked like she was doing a very uncoordinated dance move. The two laughed and hugged.

"I know that you can do this. You're already off to a great start," he replied with a genuine smile. "You've tackled the part of the book that defines who you should choose as tribe leaders and what they'll gather around, now how about the parts where he gives examples of what the tribes should be working on? What ideas do you have there?"

Leaning forward in her chair with excitement, she responded faster than she could breathe, "Godin said that the first thing a leader and their tribe leaders should do is publish a manifesto that succinctly and clearly points out what the mission of the organization is. So, I think that's the first thing that we should work on."

"That's great, but how can you be absolutely sure that your tribe leaders are on board with you on the same mission?"

"That's what we were just talking about," Carmen said proudly. "They are completely on board. They believe in students and that all students can learn at high levels given enough support. They know that our students face obstacles, but as a community, we can overcome those obstacles and ensure a bright future for our kids. We spoke deeply about it for over an hour, so I don't believe that they were just trying to please me. I think that they really believe this and they're on board. They feel like everyone at the school has been on board at one point in their career, but a long history of poor leadership and poor performance have really squashed it out of some of them."

"I am truly impressed!" he remarked even standing and giving her a one-man standing ovation out of respect. "So, what's the next step?"

"I can't think just one step ahead, so I have a few steps. First, as Godin recommends, I have to connect with my tribe leaders and make it easy for them to connect with me. Then, we have to work on that manifesto along with a powerful mission statement that we can use to guide our tribes to all row the boat in the same direction. I've decided to really go with the Pacific Northwest tribe theme with redwood tree and all." She pulled out the toy redwood tree that she purchased at a hobby store and they both laughed.

"Ok, slow down a little," he warned. "You have them on board with your mission, but before you run out and start collecting logs to carve together, be sure that you are all in agreement on possible methods for achieving your goal."

"Great point. I hadn't considered that. I have a feeling that you have something in mind," she replied looking down to see him reaching into his bag.

"But of course," he added with a grin and a fake British accent. "I had a feeling that you would have gone ahead of me and moved forward on your own. I knew for sure that you would have finished the book early. You're not the only one who thinks ahead." He winked cleverly, "I also suspected that you would have your hands full to the point that you wouldn't have had time to do any deep research yet, so I came prepared with another book."

He handed her a thick, academic looking book with charts and graphs all over the cover. It said, *"Visible Learning"* across the top and the professor must have noticed the confused look on her face.

"This one," he said, "is a little bit tougher to get through than the last two. John Hattie meta-analyzed high quality meta-analyses of educational research to determine the effect that each strategy and procedure has on students. This should be the perfect source of data for you and your tribe leaders to determine the path that you'll follow. This leadership group must focus on data and research, not bias and anecdote in order to be successful. I cannot tell you how many times I've seen a well-meaning educator argue and argue about something that they heard that their friend's cousin's school in another state did one time or something that this school used to do 25 years ago and the memory has become sweeter than the reality."

Dr. Scaffale took a deep breath and continued, "In a previous life, I worked with a math department with 3 percent proficiency who swore that many years ago, they split Algebra over 2 years and the results were much better. When pressed for data to support their claim, they realized that the results had been about the same since anyone in the room had started teaching there. It was an important lesson for them to learn about the danger of anecdotes and looking to the past through rose-colored glasses."

Carmen really bought into this idea, but her excitement subsided slightly as she said, "But I need to keep in mind Daniel Pink's idea of Mastery. I don't want 800 things to focus on. I want one or two very powerful things."

"Exactly! I want you to read this book through the lens of strategies and/or groups of strategies that are the most powerful and have the greatest probability of reaching your goals given several years of intense focus. Let me give you two weeks to digest this one. It doesn't need to be read from cover to cover, but each factor can be treated separately. Then, you can skip things that don't apply."

LEADERSHIP REFERENCE: *TRIBES*

Seth Godin's *Tribes: We Need You to Lead Us* is a short, easy read with a powerful message. Godin argues that tribes are a powerful force in reaching goals when formed around powerful ideas. Tribes still need leadership and can be strong advocates to spread messages, pilot new ideas, and brainstorm solutions. In schools, tribes are often used as an alternative to forcing everyone to try a new idea. Early adopter tribes excited about the new idea can pilot and spread their success stories with others.

Tribes flatten out the organization with distributed leadership. The book not only focuses on the actions of the tribes, but the actions that the leader has to take in order to support the tribes. The overall leader must be willing to take risks and allow the status quo to be challenged. The biggest threat to an organization with tribes throughout is a leader unwilling to let go of the reigns a bit.

Being part of a tribe is a basic human need like being hungry or thirsty. We all belong to hundreds of tribes from neighborhoods to hometowns, to religions and colleges, and to political parties and social groups. Together, they form our identity. Godin is recommending that leaders harness this natural tendency to form tribes in order to spread the mission through the organization.

Visible Learning will be discussed with chapter 6.

REFLECTION QUESTIONS

1. Who is your "tribe"? How were they selected? How do they help your organization grow?
2. How are your department chairs assigned? Is it the best way?
3. Are there examples in your organization of people seeing the past through rose-colored glasses and preventing them from trying new things?

Chapter 6

Seeing through New Eyes

Those teachers who are students of their own impact are the teachers who are the most influential in raising students' achievement.

—John Hattie

Carmen glanced down at Mrs. Toms and the other tribe leaders again and the whole crowd could see the respect and admiration that she had for them. She caught herself speechless while glancing at them and the small redwood tree that had been the source of great jokes and goofing around, yet helped them feel like a family. The tree had been on vacation in Hawaii with one of them, attended Alcoholics Anonymous meetings with another, and flew on a weather balloon as part of the class project of another. Many selfies had been taken with the redwood tree and posted on a variety of social media sites. It had become affectionately known as "Red" and if Red wasn't present for a leadership meeting, the team would scramble to find it.

Dr. Esposito continued, "In these very difficult times for me, I learned so much and I made some great friends . . . best friends. I found myself in my office one time reflecting after a particularly rewarding week. I had a friend at the county office who often called on me to go on validation visits with her for the Distinguished Schools program. After every one of about ten visits, we would have lunch and talk. Our most common conversation was, 'They did it again. It was 8:15 when the first person said that it "feels like family" to work here.'"

"We turned it into a game, pointing at our watches and smiling widely when someone said the word 'family' and without fail, it happened every time. Every single school, 10 minutes in, 15 minutes in, never more than 2 hours in, someone would say, 'It feels like family to work here.' It happened too often to just be a coincidence. These were great schools, overcoming obstacles just like we intended to do, so I knew what I had to do with these tribe leaders."

Back in the dingy, dusty meeting room, Carmen realized that one of her first tasks was to decorate this room to make it into a room where people would actually want to meet with family. And one of the things that families typically do is to eat together. She decided that she would start baking again and she would bring homemade desserts to these meetings. She would be asking them for a great deal of after-hours work and she should feed them like she would do if she had invited a cousin over to her house to fix her car. But for now, she had a room full of tribe leaders who were waiting patiently for her to begin.

She had taken just over a week to read the pertinent sections of *Visible Learning* and had already begun to digest the dense collection of information. It was the kind of book that launched her into doing further research after each section or else she would have finished it much faster. Many sections resulted in more questions than answers, but one of her favorite quotes was "A prudent question is one-half of wisdom" by Sir Francis Bacon.

"This book is the neutron star of dense educational research books," she thought to herself. She chose a handful of the more counterintuitive studies in the book and put together a pop quiz of educational strategies. She put three programs or strategies on the left and three Common Language Effect Sizes (CLE) on the right and asked the group to match them up.

She explained that Common Language Effect Sizes are a statistic that Hattie uses to show how powerful of an effect a strategy has on students. A negative CLE means that it hurt students, a CLE between 0 and 0.15 can be attributed to just growing another year older, a CLE between 0.15 and 0.40 is what teachers can accomplish without any special strategies, so a CLE greater than 0.40 is better than the best teacher could accomplish without using special strategies.

In the beginning, it was fun guessing, debating, explaining, and keeping score. Mrs. Toms, it turns out, had already read the book herself and was doing very well on the quiz. No surprise there. The final quiz question took Hattie's big categories of educational research and jumbled up their average effect sizes. The tribe leader teachers were asked to match the category with the effect size and this question could be the tiebreaker if need be. The slide looked like this:

1) Teaching Strategies   (a) 0.60
2) Curriculum   (b) 0.45
3) Teacher Characteristics   (c) 0.49
4) School   (d) 0.23
5) Home   (e) 0.31
6) Student Characteristics   (f) 0.40

The numbers were not nearly as important as the order. Carmen had the answer key in front of her and, from highest to lowest, the answer came out to be as follows:

Teaching Strategies
Teacher Characteristics
Curriculum
Student Characteristics
Home Characteristics
School Characteristics

After the joking and high fives were finished, Carmen felt like the activity hadn't generated the kind of buzz that she had hoped for but apparently it did help accomplish some of her relationship goals. Until, a serious look came across Mrs. Toms' face and she whispered quizzically, "I didn't notice that the first time."

Another voice asked, "What didn't you notice?" She replied, "Well, when you put them in order like this, something jumped out at me. What do the top two categories have in common? The teacher. Our work should have the singular focus of hiring the best teachers, training them well, motivating them to stay, and doing whatever it takes to allow them to plan and implement the best lessons anyone has ever seen." That moment was the proverbial tipping point.

Then a quiet voice, almost unfamiliar because it was so rarely heard, said, "Excellence: Every Classroom, Every Lesson, Every Day." It was Sally Moore, a social studies teacher. The room went silent for an uncomfortably long time until Mrs. Toms broke the silence with, "I lllllove it!" The tribe now had a fight song, a motto, a vision, and a change movement. This simple phrase will drive everything. But the greatest thing about it was that it was not Carmen's idea. Autonomy!

The group spent the next half an hour discussing how to advertise the new motto to teachers. They wanted to ensure that teachers know that excellence is not the same thing as perfection. Perfection is an impossible target that will only cause stress and strife. But striving for excellence creates ambition, drive, and quality. A teacher might take a risk and try something completely new in a lesson that totally flops in class. But the lesson learned makes this an excellent class and more information in the teacher's arsenal to write an even better lesson the next day. This would be an important distinction between excellence and perfection that would make or break this motto.

LEADERSHIP REFERENCE: *VISIBLE LEARNING*

John Hattie's *Visible Learning: A Synthesis of over 800 Meta-Analyses Relating to Student Achievement* in its updated form distills nearly a thousand meta-analyses of tens of thousands of studies and combines them into easy-to-understand statistics. The book tackles issues such as the effects of homework, class size, teacher education programs, and advanced degrees for teachers. This book should not be used as the definitive source of research because it just scratches the surface. Instead, it should be used as a launching point to find ideas to research more deeply. Hattie updates the data regularly, so the rankings and the effect sizes change accordingly. The book is an invaluable source of overview data to begin conversations like the one that Carmen had with her leaders.

Visible learning is not without its critics. Meta-analyses are only as good as the research that they digest. But *Visible Learning* was never meant to be the definitive guide to everything educational research. It is a starting point to launch readers into learning more. Each section has references to all of the research that was analyzed and readers should refer to those for more details on the subject. That being said, *Visible Learning* is an incredibly valuable source of conversation starters and introductions to topics in educational research.

REFLECTION QUESTIONS

1. How do you help your teachers feel like family at school?
2. Are your teachers treated as though they are the most important resource in the school?
3. How do you promote excellence in your school for all students?

Chapter 7

Influence of Gold

Trust comes from integrity. Respect comes from excellence. Loyalty comes from service. Admiration comes from an optimistic attitude.

—Chris Widener

Almost the entire original group of tribe leaders was in attendance at Carmen's retirement event. Sally Moore was the only one not in the room. Sally decided that when she retired, she would travel the world helping third world countries to build schools and she wasn't able to get away from Tanzania to make the trip. The rest of the team was now smiling and crying while they whispered fragments of stories that were currently streaming through their minds. "Remember the piñata?" "Disneyland!" and other inside jokes started circling the table. The tribe suddenly realized the effect they had on the transformation of this school. Dr. Esposito was glowing inside as she remembered these times too.

Carmen got close to the microphone again and said, "Now do you see why I don't deserve any credit for the accomplishments of this school? I didn't do any of it. It was you, the teachers, counselors, aides, supervisors, and especially you tribe leaders. Sure I went along for the ride. I hired most of you. But that was easy compared to all of the hard work that you all did interacting with students every day. When I realized that you were meeting on evenings and weekends to discuss issues, having book studies together, and speaking at school board meetings, I truly realized what a powerful change force you all are. And I will be eternally grateful to you."

When Carmen met with Professor Scaffale the next day, she told the entire story about how the meeting had gone so well, how it wasn't her idea, and how they'd come up with such a wonderful vision statement. He commented that the vision statement sounded just like golden rule #4. He expected a confused look, but instead got a smile.

Carmen got excited and said, "Now that book, I have read!"

He was referring to Chris Widener's *The Art of Influence*. Carmen had just read the book in one of her administration classes and quoted the four golden rules of leadership by heart:

(1) Live a life of undivided integrity.
(2) Always demonstrate a positive attitude.
(3) Consider other people's interests as more important than your own.
(4) Don't settle for anything less than excellence.

She could see clearly how he'd made the connection between the vision statement and golden rule #4. The professor said to her, "You know, I don't normally talk much except to ask questions. But I'd really like to get on a soapbox here. I've seen so many principals who expect their teachers to motivate students but never teach them how to motivate. They expect them to be able to collaborate with other teachers and never teach them to collaborate. They expect teachers to analyze data but never teach them how to look at data analytically. But worst of all, they expect teachers to be leaders and never teach them how to lead."

If you want this group of tribe leaders to actually be leaders, you need to teach them how to lead and this book could be the perfect start. I know that you've read the book, but have your tribe leaders read it? "One of the most powerful activities that a group of leaders can do is to discuss good books."

Carmen was pretty sure that she knew the answer to this question so she and Dr. Scaffale sat down and created a short activity to go with each golden rule in the book. Since the tribe group met once a week, they could cover the entire book in a single month. For the first golden rule, they decided to use a story right out of the book prior to reading that chapter.

The story was of a business meeting in which at one point in the story, the owner of the company told a small, relatively harmless lie in the meeting right in front of the two main characters who were considering purchasing the company. The question posed to the tribe leaders was, "Would you buy a company from this man?"

After a long conversation among the group about the data that he'd presented, the profit margins that his company was making, and other irrelevant factors, Mrs. Toms quietly said, "But he lied." The whole conversation changed at that point and went down the road of discovering golden rule #1 on their own before reading the section of the book. Carmen felt very strongly that discovery was the best way to deeply learn something.

As a former science teacher, she taught via scientific inquiry before scientific inquiry was a thing. The team was validated after reading the section from the book and seeing that the protagonist made the same decision for the same reason. But the greatest part was that Carmen didn't say a word the entire time. "Nobody washes a rental car" was one of Carmen's favorite sayings and she truly believed that ownership of an idea was extremely important to its implementation. The experience also brought the group much closer together through talking about leadership and integrity.

Integrity did not seem to be an issue with this group, but it is always an excellent regular reminder. Carmen passed along some advice that her father, the CFO of a small company, had given her numerous times, "Carmenita, before you do anything, think of how it would look on the front page of the newspaper." This fond memory of her father had guided her out of several potentially sticky situations in her career.

The next three meetings featured similarly successful activities built in and Carmen was extremely happy with how things were moving along. But that's when her phone rang. It was the nurse from her oncologist's office calling. Carmen had just had a mammogram a couple of weeks ago and the nurse requested that she come in to redo the test because there was an anomaly the first time. This is where Carmen's life came crashing down again.

LEADERSHIP REFERENCE: *THE ART OF INFLUENCE*

Chris Widener's *The Art of Influence* is a leadership lesson wrapped in a fable. The story drives home the point that good leadership is more about character than it is about skill. Throughout the book, it is made clear that great leaders are great influencers. In fact, the four golden rules of influence listed in this chapter are 100 percent about character. Each of the golden rules comes from a lesson learned by the fictional leader in the story. Although the stories are not related to educational leadership, they are readily applicable. School leaders would do well to keep the rules of influence in mind while inspiring great teachers to be excellent.

REFLECTION QUESTIONS

1. How do you express gratitude to your teachers for the great work that they do?
2. How can you work the four golden rules of leadership into your work? Which is your strength? Which do you need to work on the most?
3. How do you encourage teachers to take ownership of the school's mission and vision?

Chapter 8

The Breakthrough

The odds of hitting your target go up dramatically when you aim at it.

—Malachi Pancoast

With a glass of water now in her hand and a quivering voice, Carmen said, "As I lay in the bed in the hospital four days later with my diagnosis tear-soaked on the bedside table, I was alone. My ex-husband had moved out and I wasn't about to tell him I was going through this. I had driven away all of my friends and family with my 80-hour work weeks. I cried constantly for two days over how pitiful I had become. And then the door opened and four wonderful, familiar faces walked in. It was my tribe leaders."

"To this day, I don't know how they knew where I was or how much I needed human contact, but between the four of them, I was not alone for a minute in that room during daylight hours for the entire time that I was there. They snuck in milkshakes for me, brought me magazines, and we talked for hours. My biological family never came, but my tribe was there for me the whole time."

The three original tribe leaders who had made it to the event were going through a roller coaster of emotions while remembering wonderful stories at the same time. The tribe leaders who joined the team later knew many of the stories also and cried right along with their colleagues.

Carmen recalled when she was recovering at home after her surgery and treatment, she got a call from Mrs. Toms who said, "We have a lot of paperwork that needs your signature; can I bring them by your house for you to sign them?" Carmen responded, "No, I need to get out of the house, I'll come by the school at 3:30 so I don't cause a distraction." The forty teachers who were crowded around the speakerphone all high-fived each other when their plan worked exactly how they anticipated it would.

When Carmen came to sign the papers, she was met by all 110 of her teachers who had cards, balloons, posters, and hugs for her. She couldn't believe the support that the teachers had for her after their rocky start. And what she noticed at the center of each group of teachers was a tribe leader. It was just as Seth Godin had written; the teachers were following the tribe leaders. Her leadership was rubbing off on them and that was the greatest feeling that a leader could have. Even in her absence, the leadership team continued to guide and lead the school.

When Carmen sat down on her sofa after the homecoming event, she began to read the cards that she received. They were full of great comments and wishes of good health. But one of them made her pause. One of the teachers wrote, "We're really not the terrible teachers that you think we are. We have good hearts and we do our best."

Carmen sat and thought about this for a long while. She hated to admit to herself that she really did not think that some of her teachers were very good and this was all based upon only a handful of formal evaluations of a few new teachers. She really had not been out in classrooms very much. She vowed to make a change in this area, but she did not know how. She did know who would, though.

During her next regularly scheduled meeting with Professor Scaffale, she brought up the topic of classroom visits. He responded, "I have two ideas for you here" to which Carmen responded, "I'll bet that at least one of them is a book, right?"

Professor Scaffale pulled out his laptop and started tapping away at the keys. When he turned the screen around, it was the website for something called The Breakthrough Coach: Management Development for Instructional Leaders. It was a two-day training and, like always, she began to fill out the registration form immediately. Then she thought to ask, "What exactly is this, professor?"

Scaffale replied, "It's a training that teaches you how to set up your office, organize your schedule, work with your office manager, and handle your calendar so that you can get everything accomplished and still have hours every week to spend in classrooms. I know that it sounds unbelievable, but give it a shot." He glanced around her office and giggled. When she inquired as to what was so funny, he responded, "One of the first suggestions of the Breakthrough Coaching training is that you don't have many decorations or personal items in your office that will distract people during meetings."

Carmen glanced around her bare office walls and empty bookshelves and laughed and said, "I wish I could say that I had done it on purpose, but I hit the treadmill running when I got here and haven't stopped ever since." At the training, Dr. Esposito learned to trust her office manager to manage her calendar, preview and filter her mail and email, set up all of her meetings, and formally schedule a great deal of time for being out in classrooms.

Carmen was getting all of her work done and getting out into classrooms 2 to 4 hours per day just like Dr. Scaffale had promised. At first, she spent the out-of-office time doing traditional principal classroom observations until Professor Scaffale's next recommendation changed that for the better. With time, she began using the time even more productively.

After they spoke about it for a while and registered both Carmen and her office manager for the training, Carmen blurted out, "Oh, I just remembered, what was the second suggestion that you had for me?" Professor Scaffale flipped the computer screen around again and he had a website open with what other than a book featured on the screen. This one was called *Instructional Rounds in Education*. He added, "This will be the perfect next step for your tribe leaders and will also get you out into classrooms with a practical purpose . . . two birds, one stone."

LEADERSHIP REFERENCE: THE BREAKTHROUGH COACH

There is no book or website that can adequately describe The Breakthrough Coach methodology, the two-day training is the only option. The training was designed by Malachi Pancoast to free administrators up to have more time to get out into classrooms. The first day of the training, leaders bring a support person with them to learn the overview together. The trainer explained in one session that his daughter came home from school one day and asked, "Dad, why can't the principal be in my class all the time? My teacher is much nicer and way better when the principal is there."

This question began the mission to find a way for principals to complete the work that needed to be done all while having plenty of time to be out in classrooms. The second day, the leaders come alone to learn more about what to do with all of the extra time that their office managers are going to find for them in their schedule.

Instructional Rounds in Education will be discussed with chapter 9.

REFLECTION QUESTIONS

1. Who are your tribe leaders? How do you work together to move the mission forward?

2. What do you and your tribe leaders need to learn in order to be more effective?
3. What would it take for you to spend more time in classrooms, interacting with teachers and students?

Chapter 9

Taking a Walk

Teaching is not rocket science. It is, in fact, far more complex and demanding work than rocket science.

—Richard Elmore

Dr. Esposito was starting to get more comfortable on stage now telling stories. The memories were getting happier, so her disposition was improving also. She continued with more positive energy and more hopeful body language, "That book was the origin of the 'Learning Walks' that have become such an important piece of our school's culture. These walks spread best practices, built camaraderie, inspired some future leaders, and got me out into classrooms."

"I quickly learned from these walks that we really did have a lot of great teachers on the campus and I was holding them back with my meaningless policies, endless paperwork, and useless faculty meetings. It helped me see that if one teacher did something wrong, I made a policy for the entire school and it only served to hold back the really innovative teachers and the status quo teachers weren't going to change anyhow."

"The best way to spread the ideas from this book was to have teachers observe each other without any judgment, through the lens of spreading best practices across the school. If we were serious about our mission of 'Excellence: Every Classroom, Every Lesson, Every Day' then this was the best logical next-step. This next logical step was the guiding force leading into a cascade of other positive changes around the school and helped further develop these future leaders invested in the important work of the leadership tribe."

Chapter 9

When Dr. Scaffale next came to Carmen's office, there were posters all over her walls. "Wow, she has really digested this book thoroughly!" he thought. The first few posters that he saw read:

> Student Achievement = better content, knowledge/skills, engagement
> Must change all three
> If it's not visible, it's not there
> Performance tasks
> Learn by doing
> Description → Analysis → Prediction → Evaluation

Another poster read:

> Four Elements:
> Identify problem
> Observe
> Debrief
> Next steps

And another read:

> Launch network (tribe leaders)
> Learn to see, unlearn to judge
> Do "Learning Walks" (as we'll call them)
>
> Focus on what students are doing, not what teacher is doing
> (tasks are most important predictor)
> Facilitate
> -Careful planning
> -Four elements:
> -Set norms
> -Be a guide
> -Use questions, don't give answers
> -Focus on evidence

Professor Scaffale just stood there in amazement spinning in circles, reading the posters. "I'm astonished!" were the only words he could manage because he truly was impressed. "I am truly astonished." Carmen explained her plans to have the tribe leaders organize the schedule for the rounds, lead the walkthroughs and debriefing sessions, and she would provide substitute teachers and support as needed.

She figured that, after reading the book, the tribe leaders could train the teachers how to do the learning walks properly. It was important that these learning walks did not simply become traditional classroom walkthroughs where teachers criticized each other and focused on surface-level details.

Professor Scaffale responded, "I am genuinely impressed. You've really melded this work with your work on creating tribe leaders. I can't wait to see the first round of walkthroughs. As you read more about the process, be careful to ensure that those who are doing the instructional rounds understand that these are not nitpicking, criticizing walkthroughs as they'll probably imagine in the beginning. These are best practice, constructive learning experiences."

"These classroom visits are about determining what good teaching is by observing what students are accomplishing during the class. They are about the learner, they are not about the teacher. They are about dropping biases and open-mindedly determining if students are engaged in their learning."

He continued, "I have a question for you. You are doing a great job allowing your tribe leaders to experience autonomy. Have you considered how to extend that to the rest of the faculty? You've seen the effect that it had on the tribe leaders. Imagine that spreading across the entire school. What could you do to increase the number of people with autonomy?"

"Hmm . . . good question," she commented in order to buy herself time to think. "Let me guess, you have another book for me."

"Nope, not this time," he responded. "I'd recommend that you re-read the autonomy section of Drive, though. I've read it at least 20 times myself. I am confident that you'll come up with a solution on your own."

LEADERSHIP REFERENCE: *INSTRUCTIONAL ROUNDS*

Instructional Rounds in Education by Elizabeth City and Richard Elmore is a how-to book about facilitating classroom walkthroughs with the intent of learning and spreading best practices. The book describes the methodology to perform this form of walkthrough, caveats to keep in mind, and the negative momentum that will have to be overcome because of unhelpful walkthroughs of the past.

When implemented properly, instructional rounds can be one of the most influential practices in a school. Instructional rounds are modeled after "rounds" that doctors do through hospitals where they present a medical history and pertinent information to other doctors and medical students and they brainstorm diagnoses and treatments. But the most important part of the medical rounds is the sharing of the thinking processes and discussions of how each came to their conclusions. This is also the most important part of instructional rounds, when the group goes outside to discuss what each one saw in the classroom and what they made of it.

REFLECTION QUESTIONS

1. How could learning walks change the culture of your school?
2. What would autonomy look like across an entire school?
3. What leadership book has been your go-to when struggling with a leadership dilemma?

Chapter 10

Getting REAL

Tend to the people, and they will tend to the business.

—John Maxwell

As Dr. Esposito glanced across the crowd, she could see at least a dozen school administrators in the room. Many of them had been assistant principals, or were teachers with her who had gone on to become principals, and several were now at the district office and one at the county office. Each of them had a gift bag in front of them and one of the things they would discover inside was a copy of *Drive*.

There was a note on each copy reading, "Please pass this along to an aspiring leader in your life." They had all read it numerous times; it was more of a symbol and a reminder than anything else. It was a symbol of how much autonomy, mastery, and purpose had changed their school for the better and Carmen hoped that it could change other lives as well.

Carmen continued her story, "So, there I was again thinking that I had made great progress and realizing that I still had a lot of work to do. This was about the time that 'Professional Learning Communities' were getting off of the ground. The district had sent people to conferences and schools had changed bell schedules to make collaboration time, but it had not had much effect. Results were stagnant. There was a lot of talk in collaborative meetings, but teachers went back to their classrooms and continued to teach the way they always had. And as a result, learning stayed the same as it always had."

"The PLC conferences were inspirational, but they were high on motivation and low on how-to so teachers were just getting frustrated. The meetings were turning back into traditional department meetings. So we discussed it as a leadership team and decided to do it differently." The tribe leaders in the room chuckled at the memory because this was one of the few times that Carmen had dominated a "group decision" and had a huge impact on the conclusions. Of course, as the leader, she had the right to unilaterally make decisions and implement them as she sees best, but as an inspiration leader, this power must be wielded infrequently. Instead, motivation, inspiration, and influence are the tools of her trade.

At the next tribe leaders meeting, there were four sticky flip chart papers stuck to the walls. Carmen swallowed her pride and said to the leaders, "You all are my eyes and ears out there. You help me spread motivation and strive to live our mission every day. You each have the potential to be great leaders. But if you're going to be leaders, I need to give you something to lead."

"I would like each of you to choose an area that you're passionate about improving at this school and lead a group that will help address that area. Then you put together your own teams of teachers to make advisory committees to field questions and make decisions related to your respective areas of passion. These groups will become the decision-making process at the school." Carmen was not the one to delegate responsibility and had a list of excuses why she did everything herself. "I don't want to be a burden." "It's my job, not theirs." "I'm a servant leader." "It would take me longer to explain it than to just do it myself."

Immediately, she heard, "I'm great at writing grant proposals and overseeing projects so I'd love to lead a group like that." That was followed up by, "My passion is student learning, real, long-lasting learning so I could lead a group on that." Almost at the same time, two other tribe leaders spoke up, one saying, "I had such a great time on the Sunshine Committee that I'd love to lead a group that works on the school culture and environment for both students and teachers," and the other said "This is the age of achievement. I'd love to lead a committee on assessment, accountability, and data."

There was excitement in the room, excitement about truly being a leader at the school as well as excitement about working on a passion project. Some tech companies give employees time to work on passion projects from one day a month to one day a week. Google reports that when they were a startup, they offered employees time to work on passion projects every Friday and called it 20 percent time. Even though their passion project Friday was only 20 percent of their time, it resulted in projects that contributed far more than 20 percent of their income. Carmen was hoping to utilize some of this energy to improve the school.

Carmen responded, "Wow, that's perfect. We can sit down with a list of teachers and have you invite teachers who you'd like to work with to be on your committee. Now when, say, someone contacts me with an idea for a grant, I'll send it to the resources group to decide how to handle it. If someone calls with a proposal for an anti-bullying campaign, I'll connect them with the environment group. When it comes time to update our pyramid of interventions, the achievement group can meet to discuss it. And when we need to decide whether to buy laptops, Chromebooks, or tablets, the lifelong learning group can research the issue."

Then it struck her, "Hey! Resources, Environment, Achievement, and Life-Long Learning, let's call them REAL Committees."

They spent the rest of the meeting excitedly planning what they would do next. By the end of the meeting, agendas had been written, lists were made, events were planned, and leaders were excited. "This autonomy, mastery, and purpose thing really works!" she thought to herself. This was only the tip of the iceberg for the REAL Committees.

LEADERSHIP REFERENCE

No leadership books were referenced in this chapter.

REFLECTION QUESTIONS

1. How effective are collaborative meetings at your school? How much could instruction improve if the collaborative time was more productive?
2. How do you allow teachers to pursue their passions?
3. How much decision-making power do your teachers have? Your teacher leaders?

Chapter 11

Flipping 360 Degrees

To add value to others, one must first value others.

—John Maxwell

"That was another day that would define the trajectory of our school. The Instructional Rounds were great, but adding these truly autonomous groups on top of them really made a vast difference in culture, motivation, and student achievement." Dr. Esposito continued, "Friendships were formed, the relationship between myself and the teachers improved, and student learning skyrocketed." There was an overall unanimous agreement across the room. Some of Carmen's changes were met with resistance, but not this one.

"These committees practically took over the school. Nearly all important decisions were routed through one or more of the groups. They designed new programs, raised money, created school events, instituted school-wide instructional change, planned spirit days, implemented interventions, hosted professional development sessions, and so much more. And it all happened without me even raising a finger. They had a life of their own and that life was pumping positive culture through the school."

There really was almost instantaneous positive change when this strategy was implemented. It just went to show that bottom-up leadership really can work. "This is the point in my career that I really started developing the leaders already in my school and learning that I didn't have to do everything . . . that it was ok to let go. I also learned that it is ok to give credit to those leaders who were doing the work. Credit for a job well-done is not a finite resource. Giving credit to another person does not take anything away from me. One candle loses nothing by lighting another candle and the world . . . or the school . . . becomes a brighter place."

Chapter 11

Carmen was at her desk signing purchase orders, scheduling expulsion hearings, and all of the other things that consume a principal's day when Mrs. Toms walked in. "Carmen, I have a huge favor to ask of you. My team is on the verge of a breakthrough. We have a schedule of parent meetings for next year, an anti-bullying campaign planned, digital end-of-year surveys accessible through a QR code, and a whole list of additional awards that we'd like to offer." She was almost out of breath, she was so excited.

"But, we need three things. First, we need more time. One meeting a month isn't enough. We'd like to convert one of our department meetings a month into another REAL committee meeting. I'm not supposed to tell you this, but we'd be willing to add another meeting to the schedule altogether to get this work done." "We are really caught up in the mission to improve the school from the inside out."

"Second, we realized that our activities overlap with the other three committees and we need time to co-plan. We thought that maybe we could have half of the leadership team meeting to spend on coordination. Finally, if you really want us to be leaders, let us plan the faculty meetings. We can spend the other half of the leadership team meetings planning the faculty meetings."

Mrs. Toms took a deep breath, winked, and said, "Of course, you're still invited to the leadership team meetings, but just as a consultant. I guess that means that fourth of all, we need to take over planning of the leadership team meetings too."

Carmen was absolutely glowing inside! But, she didn't want to reveal how happy she was about this turn of events, so she tried as hard as she could to hold back her grin and she said, "Well, I'll need some time to think about this and I'm going to have to run it by the other team leaders to see if they agree. If so, we might have to put the change of department meeting to a vote of the whole faculty." As any good leader would, Mrs. Toms had already run the idea past the other leaders who had already run it by their teams and she already knew that they were all on board.

Carmen asked Mrs. Toms to close the door for a moment and spent 20 minutes telling her how proud she is of the leadership role she is taking, the work that she is accomplishing, and the zest for this new work that she is exhibiting. Mrs. Toms explained, "Every time we say this, we knock on wood, but we are really glad that you're here and we hope that you stay for a very long time. We haven't had a leader like you in . . . ever. I hope this isn't weird, but we love you like family." This was music to Carmen's ears.

Carmen said to Mrs. Toms, "Someone has changed my life by suggesting great books for me to read and I have one that I'd like to suggest to you." She leaned back in her chair and slid a book out from between some of the other books Dr. Scaffale had suggested which were now taking up almost an entire shelf in her bookcase.

Mrs. Toms glanced at the cover and said, "360° Leader, I think I know what it's about from the title, but is there anything specific you'd like me to focus on?" Carmen replied, "You've shown great passion for leadership as a Tribe Leader. You have the relationship-building skills as well as the emotional intelligence to be a great leader. Many people think that leaders are born, not created. But, I believe that great leadership is a set of skills and habits that can be learned. Certainly, these skills come more naturally to some than others and you seem to be a natural."

"This book will be your first step to formal leadership. I hope that someday, you decide to go into administration, but this book explains how to be a leader from right where you are. Let's discuss it when you're finished. This book has helped me with my leadership and I wish that I'd read it sooner. One of the leadership myths that he covers is that I'll learn to be a good leader when I get a leadership position."

"You are in a position now to start learning about leadership BEFORE you get into a formal leadership position and I want to help you do that." Carmen felt like she was preaching now and figured that some of John Maxwell's speaking style may have rubbed off on her.

"I hope that I've relieved some of the 360 degree leader tension by empowering you and giving you parameters for your work. You will likely struggle with the 'many-hats' challenge, but you are efficient and communicate with me well so I believe that we can overcome that together. I will need your help with something, however."

"One of the least fulfilling things about being a 360 degree leader is when the positional leader gets all of the credit for the great work that you do. I don't want to be that leader and I need your help to ensure that I spread the credit around. I promise that I will make it my mission to give credit and take blame as I work to develop this team into leaders."

Mrs. Toms was so excited about the news that the leadership team was going to be taking on new responsibilities, that she really didn't hear everything that Carmen was saying. She replied, "OK, I can help you with that"? and got up from her chair. As Mrs. Toms scurried out of the room, book in hand, to go tell her team the news, Carmen relaxed back into her chair. She had the biggest smile on her face since she met Matthew McConaughey at a gift shop in Beverly Hills ten years ago. Things were really starting to come together.

LEADERSHIP REFERENCE: *THE 360 DEGREE LEADER*

The 360 Degree Leader: Developing Your Influence from Anywhere in the Organization by John Maxwell sets the case for how important middle-level leaders are to any organization. Although it is used here with a teacher's leadership, principals, directors, and assistant superintendents are all 360 degree leaders as well and can learn from the lessons within.

Maxwell identifies seven myths about leading from within, mostly centered around the idea that one can become a leader after they get a leadership position. Although there is a lot of on-the-job learning in a school leadership position, one would never decide to learn electrical engineering after getting an electrical engineering job and should not do so with a leadership position either. Maxwell then identifies seven challenges of leading from the middle. Many of the challenges deal with how difficult it is to lead when someone else is making the decisions, especially if that person is not an effective leader.

Maxwell separates leading up (influencing those above you) from leading across (leading peers) and leading down (traditional idea of leadership). He identifies nine principles of leading up and they really boil down to building relationships, supporting your leader, and being reliable. There are seven principles of leading across and the important aspects include building relationships and avoiding unnecessary politics and competition. There are seven principles of leading down which really focus on being seen, being fair, and building capacity.

REFLECTION QUESTIONS

1. What would your teachers change about your school if they had only one wish? How can you make that change happen without discovering a magic lamp?
2. How can you get your staff more involved in planning and implementing change in your school?
3. How do you help support the learning of aspiring administrators and 360 degree leaders?

Chapter 12

A Simple Plan

The fundamental purpose of school is learning, not teaching.

—Richard DuFour

Dr. Esposito continued her story while she brushed away the thick memories from in front of her face, "Of course, the vote of the leadership team was unanimous on all counts and the vote of the faculty got every vote except one." Suddenly, a balding teacher in the back of the room stood up and called out with a smile, "OK, give me the ballot back, I'll change my vote!"

The whole room broke out into laughter because if they were to bet on who that one vote was, they would have bet on Chuck without a doubt. Dr. Esposito continued, "Over the next 3 years, test scores went up, graduation rates climbed, morale improved, but something was still missing because we weren't reaching all students."

"There were still gaps. They were shrinking, but they were still present and persistent. We pored over the data and were happy because proficiency rates were increasing and graduation rates were improving, but some kids ended up on the bottom of those measures each year, often the same kids over and over. We were not doing enough to fix this."

"The Achievement team in the REAL committees had collected some data that was not surprising, but still telling. All of our subgroups' data had improved, but there were two particular groups performing significantly lower than others and this bothered me. I was happy to be almost up to the district average overall, but I was still unhappy with the persistent gaps. We vowed that all students would learn at high levels, it was in our Mission Statement, and we weren't fulfilling that vow."

Chapter 12

Carmen thought to herself, "I knew it couldn't last forever." "It" was peace on the leadership team. She was sitting in the middle of a knockdown, drag-out fight that she, herself, had accidentally started. She started the argument by asking the question, "If we truly believe that all kids can learn, why are we leaving so many kids behind?"

She really wished for the ability to reach out into the air and take a question back, but it was too late for that. She had passed out data showing the number of "Did Not Meet Standard" test scores at the school. Although there was too much chaos to catch everything that was said, she heard things like "So, you're blaming this on us?" followed by "We can lead a horse to water . . . but we cannot make them think!" and then, "I can't believe you've been using us. All this time we've been working together and you still think that we're the problem!" Two years of relationship building out the window with just one ill-framed question.

She learned near the end of her first marriage that when someone is angry, you should give them ample time to vent before intervening, so she let the tirade go on for a little while and then calmly jumped in. "I am not saying this is your fault or even that it is the fault of one single person or group, parents, society, the district, the state, textbook publishers, politicians, social media. But what I do know is that no matter whose fault it is, teachers are the only ones who have the power to fix this. We cannot fix society, we cannot fix parents, we cannot fix video games, we cannot fix societal systemic racism, and we cannot fix poverty. We we can do our damnedest to fix student learning, which, in turn, fixes many of those things."

She let that comment just sit in the air for a moment, not knowing exactly how it would be taken. There wasn't even any breathing in the room. Carmen could hear the old clock on the wall ticking seconds away as they all sat in uncomfortable silence. If her heart was actually beating, she probably could have heard that, too.

The comment was an empowering comment, yet scary at the same time. It was a mixture of responsibility and power all rolled together. Mrs. Toms then said, "You know, she's right. Carmen can't fix this, parents won't fix this, and politicians sure as hell can't fix this. These kids have the best parents that they are ever going to get. We're the only ones with the power and the will to change these kids' lives."

She continued nervously, but passionately, "We all feel proud and accept credit for their successes on awards night and at graduation, so we as a community also have to take some sense of partial responsibility for their failures. It wouldn't be fair to take one without the other. We spend more waking hours with these kids than any other person, including their parents in most cases. It's not our fault when they fail but it is our responsibility to do everything within our power to ensure that they succeed."

Then Sally Moore, the quiet social studies teacher spoke up. "If we're going to do this, then we need to redesign our Professional Learning Community time." She went on to explain that at her last school, they did Professional Learning Communities (PLCs) without much effect because a few teachers went to a conference, time was scheduled, and data was analyzed, but it never went any farther than that. In other words, it never affected what happened in the classroom.

What she said next set the rest of the team back in their chairs a little, "If our PLCs are not changing what the adult at the front of the room is doing, then we are spinning our wheels. We can change bell schedules and create pretty charts and graphs, but if teaching doesn't change, then learning doesn't change either."

"We saw how important teachers and teaching are in the Visible Learning book and our PLCs are not affecting either one of them. I have sat in dozens of these meetings, made agreements, and then went on teaching like I always have. I cannot speak for everyone, but I am embarrassed to say that nothing has changed in my classroom in two years of collaborating with my peers." Several "Me neither" responses circulated the room as the tension started to relax a little.

Together, they finished the meeting peacefully and created a four-year plan for how to implement effective PLCs based upon Sally's experience at her previous school The simple plan read as follows:

Year 1:

- Take teachers through the *Visible Learning* quiz to discover how powerful teachers are.
- Set *all* PLC time aside for writing collaborative lesson plans.
- One of a kind teachers get together to collaborate around strategies.
- Don't even call it PLC because the acronym has become tainted by improper implementation.

Year 2:

- Ask, "How do we know if our lessons worked?"
- Create common assessments over essential standards to measure how the lessons are working. Use a variety of measures, not simply multiple choice assessments.
- Use PLC time almost exclusively for creating assessments, formative and summative.

Year 3:

- Ask, "How do we use the data we've collected to ensure that all students are learning?"
- Create a template for analyzing common assessment data.
- Use PLC time for analyzing data from assessments, analyzing student work, etc.

Year 4:

- Ask, "What should we do when a student didn't learn the material?"
- Ask, "How do we extend learning for those who do master the standard the first time?"
- Design intervention and enrichment activities

Mrs. Toms pointed out that this series of events was in perfect alignment with a book she'd just read about PLCs called *Learning by Doing*. It called for answering three questions in PLCs: "What do we want kids to learn?" followed by "How will we know if they have learned it?" and "What do we do if they don't learn it?" But this four-year plan was a no-pressure method for implementing PLCs without rushing through . . . allowing time for mastery . . . before moving on to the next question.

Mrs. Toms pointed out that, just like Sally, at her previous school, they tried to tackle all of these things at once and none of them ever got accomplished. Treating them one at a time and giving a year to figure them out before moving on to the next one seemed like a much better idea. Carmen grinned as she realized how she was going to accomplish "mastery" now.

Their schedule addressed the first PLC question ("What do we want students to learn?") through a conversation where they determined that it's impossible to collaboratively plan every lesson, design common assessments for every standard, and analyze data from this myriad of assessments. So, they decided to focus their collaboration time on the most important standards. Collaborative teams only met approximately twenty-four times per year and there were more than fifty content standards, so it would be impossible to thoroughly collaborate around every single standard. Out of necessity, they would have to narrow down the list.

The team could not decide what to call those standards, but agreed that it was a good idea to narrow it down. In fact, they spent more than an hour just debating what to call the standards; essential standards, power standards, and many other options were considered, each with its own connotations and baggage. Once they decided what to call them, the really difficult work began, figuring out which standards are most important. The district office had already identified power standards. The assistant superintendent sat in a room alone and used the blueprints for the state test to determine which standard was most important solely by how many questions were on the state test.

This practice led to a long debate about whether the blueprint was an effective way to identify important standards or not. English teachers seemed to think that it was a good way because they explained that English is a skills-based course. Science and math teachers thought that it was not a good method because concepts build upon each other.

The conversation started to get heated again until the chemistry teacher stood up. She asked Carmen to pull up the standard about "moles" and the blueprint for that standard. She said, "According to the blueprint, there is only one direct question about the mole so the assistant superintendent identified that as very low on the importance list. But if students don't understand the mole, they won't understand concentration, dilution, distillation, balanced equations, stoichiometry, gas laws, pH, equilibrium, electric potential, or anything else. Just those topics alone add up to 18 questions on the exam."

A hush fell across the room until Mrs. Toms asked, "I think that we can agree that the number of test questions is a poor way to identify important standards. Then how should we identify which standards are essential?" and the conversation began to move in a different direction.

As a staff, they decided that Larry Ainsworth's idea of Endurance, Leverage, and Readiness would be their criteria for an essential standard. Each standard would go through a three-stage filter: is it critical in life, is it critical later in this class, and/or is it critical in another class. They were excited and the chemistry teacher felt relieved that "moles" met the Readiness criteria and that she could spend more time on the important topic.

The freedom from using the district's list of power standards was great, but the autonomy that teachers had to develop their own list of essential standards instead of depending on an assistant superintendent to do it gave them the ownership to actually make use of the list. Carmen felt like she had accomplished two missions: providing autonomy and creating tribe leaders.

The second PLC question ("How will we know if they have learned it?") was addressed by the common lesson planning and common formative assessments. In the end, the team spent several years agreeing on and perfecting common assessments and another year or two figuring out how to analyze the data well. But Carmen was not concerned about the timeline. This is how "mastery" works. Teachers must be given ample time to become an expert in one thing before moving on to put out the next fire. Teachers were relieved to be able to focus on one thing at a time and to continue to focus on it until they had mastered that skill.

The third PLC question would also take much longer than expected. The team imagined a simple system of interventions and tutoring to fix the "What do we do if they don't learn it?" question, but things are rarely as simple as they seem. This part of the transformation would reveal the epitome of learning by doing in action.

LEADERSHIP REFERENCE: *LEARNING BY DOING*

Learning by Doing: A Handbook for Professional Learning Communities at Work by the late Richard DuFour is the closest thing there is to a manual on how to implement PLCs. Most of the other books are theoretical, but this one is practical. The chapters include things like "Establishing a Focus on Learning," "Creating Team-Developed Common Formative Assessments," and "Responding When Some Students Don't Learn." It is the road map for a school beginning to develop a collaborative culture or struggling to move from collaborative meetings to a collaborative school culture.

Learning by Doing responds to the three PLC questions with specific strategies for setting up a school that uses collaborative time to answer them. Because every school is different, it would be impossible to prescribe universal answers to the questions, but strategies are given to help schools discover their own answers. DuFour also recommends the idea of loose-tight leadership where a leader determines which factors are critical to success at their school and are tight in requiring those things and loose on everything else.

REFLECTION QUESTIONS

1. What persistent achievement gaps are there at your school? What are you doing to address them?
2. How are you putting deposits in your emotional bank account so that you have some buffer in your relationships in case you slip up?
3. In what areas of your school are your teachers afforded autonomy? How can you increase the number of areas?

Chapter 13

Positive Deviance

Look vigilantly for one or two actions that create a cascade of change.

—Joseph Grenny

"This was another one of those plant-a-flag-on-the-moon moments that changed the direction of the school. This single meeting was responsible for our common assessments, shared folders on Google Drive, data-based Learning Walks, annual data presentations, online common testing, common policies on grading and homework, and much, much more."

"Not only did these PLCs result in all of these tangible products, but they resulted in a plethora of non-tangible products as well. Rapport with a variety of colleagues improved, positive school culture for both adults and students boosted through the roof, classroom instruction was refined and focused, and student overall contentedness could be felt by anyone on campus."

The audience could see her eyes move upward as she started to recall these distant memories, "I remember once when I was doing a 1-year follow-up with a student after a suspension for a fight that he was in. I congratulated him on not having gotten into any trouble this year—which was a huge accomplishment for this young man." Carmen could see the crowd leaning over, whispering to each other, trying to figure out who she was talking about and what was coming next.

"I asked him, 'What made the difference for you?' He responded immediately without even thinking about it, 'I just don't hate coming to school anymore.' These were joyous words to my ears and nothing could have made me feel more that the work that we were doing was worthwhile. This was the kind of student who would be last to be impacted by changes in a school and he had definitely been positively impacted. Test scores were improving, and the graduation rate was up, but this made me feel even better. I felt good that we were reaching the vast majority of our student body."

Carmen paused and added, "The culture change was great and largely invisible from the outside. But what won us awards for our amazing results was the 'Interrichment' program that grew from these conversations."

Mrs. Toms pointed out at the May leadership team meeting that this was the annual "How well are we progressing towards our goals?" meeting. Each department was to present a poster board that they had created, something like a science fair project. The presentation reiterated their goals for the year, provided trend data from common assessments, and charted summative data compared to their goals and previous classes of students. It could be as creative or as informative as they chose.

Carmen was a big believer in the idea that the best way to improve anything is to observe good examples of it. She had just finished a book that Mrs. Toms had recommended to her, *Influencer: The New Science of Leading Change*, which had a whole chapter on this. Joseph Grenny and colleagues called it "studying positive deviance" and that is exactly what was going on here.

They were all set up in the faculty lunch room and the posters had become very elaborate with well-analyzed data and thoughtful analyses. Many included samples of student work that had been analyzed with common rubrics by groups of teachers. There was test score data, attendance data, survey data, course grades, standardized test scores, and so much more. The posters were set up for a week and lunch was provided for teachers each day that week to entice them to eat in the faculty room where the projects were set up. Then, each team presented their data to the entire faculty over a span of several faculty meetings. It felt like a medical seminar where doctors did poster presentations and then had panel discussions following.

Although there was presently no math teacher on the leadership team, the math presentation was most impressive of all. Carmen could vividly remember her first meeting with the math teachers her very first year. She held data in her hands that almost made her cry. She said to them, "You're math teachers. If 3% of our students are proficient, how many students is that?" No answer.

"If 97% of our students are not proficient and 15% of our students tested into the Gifted Program, what does that say about our math instruction?" No answer. "What are we going to do?" she asked. She almost blew a gasket when a lone response came back, "That's just our students. It's always been that way and it always will be."

So much had changed since then. The rest of that math department meeting was a frustrating list of excuses why students cannot learn mathematics.

Teachers reflected back nearly ten years when they had attempted to spread algebra over two years and recalled how incredibly successful it was. As the story went, the evil district office banned the practice and math teachers were furious about it for all of the years since then.

When Carmen pulled up the data (which was public data available to everyone) to show that for the last fifteen years, Algebra 1 test scores had hovered between 2 percent and 4 percent and there was no evidence that at any time any intervention had improved these numbers, two of the math teachers stormed out of the room as their house of cards began to fall.

It was almost unfathomable how far the math department had come along in just a couple of years. Two years ago, they were resistant to change and unwilling to consider self-improvement. Today, they were delivering a highly professional presentation to an audience that included department chairs from two other schools. The relationship that the tribe leaders had built, the trust that had developed, and the influence strategies had much to do with the transition.

Pride glowed off of the pages of their presentations. Student achievement was vastly improved, attendance was up, discipline was down, morale had completely turned around, teacher transfer requests were almost nonexistent, and the number of parents requesting to transfer their children to other schools was at nearly zero.

Then Carmen threw out the word "But . . ." and paused for several seconds. "We still haven't accomplished our mission of intervening for all kids who need it or providing enrichment for those who get it already. We've tried Saturday school, we've tried after school tutoring, we've even tried voluntary cross-age tutoring. They've all helped a little, but have not accomplished the mission. Kids didn't show up for Saturday school, most students have jobs and cannot come after school. We need to find another way."

Mrs. Toms, brilliant as always, was presenting her department's data that day. It was clear that she had been considering Carmen's words. She concluded her brilliant 35-minute presentation by saying, "The only way that we can make intervention and enrichment work is if it is mandatory and the only way to make it mandatory is to make it within the school day. But I don't know how to do that." It got everyone thinking, mostly thoughts about how disruptive and difficult something such as that would be.

Mrs. Moore replied, "Leave that to me. We're studying school schedules in my admin class right now and I'll have a plan by next time." A look of shock and awe spread around the table since nobody knew that Mrs. Moore was even interested in administration, never mind enrolled in an admin program. When Carmen did consider the notion, she realized that Mrs. Moore would make a great administrator. She had all of the traits of a good leader. She was a servant leader with very good emotional intelligence and she would give the jacket off of her back on a cold day for a needy student. She was just so quiet that nobody had ever thought about it before.

LEADERSHIP REFERENCE: *INFLUENCER*

Influencer: The New Science of Leading Change by Joseph Grenny, Kerry Patterson, and colleagues is one of the greatest books about implementing change in an organization, a community, or the world. The influencer framework is described in detail with examples of projects of many different sizes in many places around the world that have used the strategies to influence great change. The examples range from eradicating the guinea worm in Africa to losing weight and rehabilitation of criminals.

The first key component of the Influencer Change Framework is clarifying measurable and important results. It is no good to work for years on an immeasurable, unimportant, or ineffective goal. The book describes what good results indicators look like with real world examples. Next is to figure out a small number (typically three) of vital behaviors necessary to make the change. For example, research has shown that for losing weight, the three vital behaviors are: weigh yourself every day, exercise at home, and eat breakfast. Although those things alone will not guarantee weight loss, the vast majority of people who lost significant weight and kept it off followed those three habits.

One of the ways to find vital behaviors is to study "positive deviance" or those who succeed where most others are not. There are papers about 90/90/90 schools, books like *It's Being Done*, and local standout schools that can be studied. But it is rare for a school to reach out and study others. Another option is to study positive deviance within the school. That is where learning walks come in. Teachers can learn from master teachers and spread effective strategies schoolwide. The poster presentations were another form of studying positive deviance. Every department has something great that they're doing and in a collaborative school, that number should grow annually. That is the power of studying positive deviance.

REFLECTION QUESTIONS

1. What does your school do for enrichment? For intervention? Are you doing enough for these two groups?
2. How do teachers and departments at your school share data and best practices with each other?
3. How might strict adherence to your school schedule and calendar be holding you back from accomplishing your goals?

Chapter 14

By Name and by Need

There is no greater accomplishment for mentors than when people they develop pass them by!

—John Maxwell

Carmen was much more excited now that the story was getting more positive and uplifting. "I forgot to mention that the day of our Leadership Team meeting with the data presentations was also my formal evaluation day." The crowd erupted in a playful "Booooooooo." "Earlier that week, the assistant superintendent, whose name I'm struggling to recall, told me that she'd like to meet with me in two days and have the superintendent present at the meeting."

"This superintendent was celebrity-status, like kiss-the-ring style. He never visited campuses and certainly never sat in on meetings. I called my boyfriend at the time and told him to search our portable hard drives for my resume because I was getting fired for sure. We even called to see how difficult it would be to get out of the lease on our new car. Of course, I cried for 2 days, blamed myself, and was depressed just like I always do in these situations."

"It turned out to be quite the contrary, the assistant superintendent came to my office to tell me that she was retiring and she wanted me to be her replacement. She had a transition plan and a salary offer all prepared when I arrived. And she brought the celebrity superintendent to try to be more convincing. She pushed the contract over to me with a pen fully expecting me to sign on the spot and be thrilled about it. It was almost as if this was part of the process, put a few years in at the struggling school and you'll be rewarded."

The room buzzed in anger since nobody had ever heard this story before. "Of course I said no. It was like my neighbors who I hardly know asking me if I'd like to abandon my own family and join theirs. You should have seen the confused looks on their faces!" All of the facial expressions in the room read the exact same emotion, "Of course you said no."

Mrs. Moore came back to the next meeting with a self-authored, twenty-seven-page paper with color charts and graphs entitled "By Name and By Need: Providing Intervention and Enrichment within the School Day." She had emailed it in advance to all of the teachers on the team and was a little embarrassed that she forgot to send it to Carmen. In Carmen's eyes, this was the best compliment she could receive, proof that they really didn't need her anymore. In her mind, this was the true measure of great leadership. She felt like her job was to get out of their way, remove as many obstacles as possible, and let them do their thing and it was working.

The REAL Committees had taken off and were leading the school. Large numbers of teachers were taking on leadership roles; decision-making was being shared; and the school was addressing all three areas of autonomy, mastery, and purpose. Carmen had very little involvement in it all except in a support role. The irony began to hit her that she encouraged her teachers to be student-centered, but as a leader, she was not teacher-centered—until now.

By the end of the meeting, Mrs. Moore's research summary and proposal had been turned into a practical guide for implementation. The plan that the teachers collaboratively developed was to add three days to the pacing guide after each common assessment. Students who scored proficient on the essential standards would go to one classroom for enrichment activities such as experiments, projects, debates, competitions, cross-age tutoring, video production, and more. These activities were always curriculum related and engaging at the same time.

Students who were not proficient on the assessment would spend two days in intervention and one day retaking the exam. The interventions often included cross-age tutoring; reciprocal teaching; computerized, targeted reteaching, and re-instruction in a different format or by a different teacher. But even more importantly, they would track how the students performed on the second exam and compare it to the first exam in order to measure how well the interventions were working.

They had created a color-coded spreadsheet that highlighted improvements in green, decreases in red, and those who stayed the same were highlighted in yellow. They obsessed over this data as well as numerous other sources to affect as many students as possible with their interventions.

Carmen was highly impressed that they were implementing things, measuring the effectiveness, and modifying and then repeating that process again. Because of this thorough process, they realized that the classroom instruction wasn't yet perfect and was overwhelming the interventions.

This realization reinvigorated their collaboration time where they would now focus on taking some of the powerful strategies used in their interventions and motivational strategies used in their enrichment and weaving them into their classrooms every day. They realized that if these were truly best practices, then they should be using them in their daily instruction.

After several rounds of measuring and modifying, they found that the biggest factor affecting the success of the program was to have the most successful teachers with the intervention students. This was almost heresy in education where experienced teachers "earn" the right to only teach advanced curriculum to highly motivated students and rookie teachers are given the most difficult assignments.

Carmen was pleased to hear that the conversations focused on solutions instead of problems or justifications. She truly liked where this was going and the synergy between autonomous tribes, learning walks, and now the work with interventions and enrichment felt like things were headed in the right direction for once.

This synergy reminded her of a quote from one of the favorite John Maxwell books she read in her credential program, "The people closest to me determine my level of success or failure. The better they are, the better I am. And if I want to go to the highest level, I can do it only with the help of other people. We have to take each other higher." The people around her were getting very, very good and Carmen was getting better each day about getting out of their way and letting them be excellent.

Mrs. Toms blurted out at the meeting, "Oh, no, I forgot that I have a guest who wanted to speak to us today. He's been sitting outside the whole time!" She rushed out the door and walked back in next to a burly man with shorts and a school baseball cap. It was the physical education (PE) department chair, Mr. O'Grady.

Mr. O'Grady exchanged pleasantries with the group and said, "I'll just get right down to it. My department is frustrated with the PLCs. We walked around that room of display boards and we were embarrassed. We are great teachers who want to do right by our students, but we are being overlooked and we are not being given any opportunities to contribute."

The entire leadership team glanced around at each other, guilty looks on their faces. They had overlooked the PE department and now saw the error in their ways. The science department chair, Mrs. Carole, got out of her seat and said, "We apologize. We did overlook you and that was a huge mistake. You all are very important to this school; PE and sports is the only reason that some students come to school." She was walking toward a centerpiece on another table that had balloons, flowers, and candy in it. She untied the balloon and began walking toward Mr. O'Grady.

As Mrs. Carole walked toward him, she said, "We will not make this mistake again. We want to put you on display as the wonderful, valuable teachers that you are." As she said that, she began to tie a balloon to the button on top of his baseball cap. "This is a symbol that you all will never be invisible again."

Mr. O'Grady was baffled. He had expected a fight. He had expected insults. His department had never gotten any respect from the other departments who really did not know what a PE teacher does every day. The science department chair continued, "We understand how important you are. We understand how important physical activity is to our students. We understand how difficult it is to have class sizes of 100 or more. And we understand how you might feel a lack of respect since there is no state testing in PE and core subjects get all of the attention. But be assured that we respect you and we are going to make sure that in the future you are included in our conversations."

Mrs. Carole adopted the PE department and attended several of their department meetings to begin to learn more about what they do. She included them in leadership activities and found them to be excellent teachers who care about students and want to be more involved. But they were rarely asked to be more involved. At the next faculty meeting, there was a table full of PE teachers, all with balloons floating above their baseball caps. They contributed more, they were happier, they felt like part of the school. They belonged.

LEADERSHIP REFERENCE: *MENTORING 101*

John Maxwell's *Mentoring 101* is part of a series of "101" books for leaders on leadership, attitude, teamwork, success, self-Improvement, and relationships. The books can be read in any order as long as *Relationships 101* comes first. Maxwell spends a great deal of effort in *Mentoring 101* expressing that before a leader can mentor another, they must have a trusting relationship. The books are short and peppered with stories to drive the lessons home with great quotes from other historical leaders.

The mentoring book goes on to lay out how to set up a mentorship, establishing trust, areas to support, and sharing failures. Maxwell believes that people learn as much or more from failures than successes. But, it seems, leaders are afraid to share their failures with others. This leads to an impossible pursuit of perfection that will only lead to frustration.

REFLECTION QUESTIONS

1. It has been said that you can tell the value of an employee by how hard you would fight if they told you they were leaving? Which teachers would you fight for? What are you doing to keep them happy?
2. What do you currently offer voluntarily after school that should be mandatory within the school day?
3. Who at your school is invisible and being overlooked as a resource? What can you do to involve them?

Chapter 15

Bottom Up When Possible, Top Down When Necessary

Feedback is oxygen. It's lifeblood. We can't grow and develop without it.

—Roger Conners

"That certainly wasn't the end of the quest to perfect 'inter-richment' as it came to be called. It went through many changes before becoming what it is today. Our proficiency rate was again boosted and our course failure rate plummeted as a result of this idea. This led to higher graduation and college-going rates as well and a host of other cascade effects. At least it had that effect on the departments that chose to use it. And then there was social studies." A joking rumble passed through the room and everyone turned to see the social studies teachers hiding behind their giant clipboards.

"The social studies department decided that inter-richment was not going to prepare students for college where students are never allowed a second chance. I remember a conversation with Dr. Scaffale where we discussed the idea that follows the line of reasoning that if we are to prepare students for college, we must give them small doses of college in high school."

"It seems to be a common conversation around the teacher's lounge, 'Why do you give so much homework? Because they're going to have a lot of homework in college. Why don't you accept late work? College professors don't accept late work.' Professor Scaffale had just read a book called 'What Great Principals do Differently' that pointed out that this same logic could be used to justify beer and pornography in high school. I, myself, believe that the best way to prepare a student for college is not to use the same flawed strategies they'll see in college, but instead to teach them well."

Chapter 15

Mrs. Moore rushed into the office Tuesday after collaboration time. She plopped down in the chair across the desk from Carmen clearly distressed about something and unable to make eye contact. When Carmen began to ask what was wrong, Mrs. Moore held up one finger asking for her to wait while she tried to hold back her tears. Carmen knew better than to try to move too quickly with an emotional person, a lesson that she learned too late in her marriage. She waited patiently planning a variety of next moves depending on what came from Mrs. Moore next.

Finally, Sally blurted out, "I don't think I want to be department chair anymore. I'm tired of having the lowest proficiency rate in the school! I'm tired of dealing with the members of my department who are jaded, and I'm tired of being the only one in the department who realizes how poorly our department is doing." She paused and swallowed with difficulty.

"Today, when I showed our most recent common assessment data, they didn't care that we were tied for the lowest department in the school, they didn't care that we are the lowest social studies department in the district, and they didn't care that we haven't improved in three years. I don't know how to deal with this. I've tried motivation and it's not working. What do I do? I'm ready to give up!"

Carmen calmed Mrs. Moore as much as she could and promised her a solution, but honestly did not know what that solution would be at this point. Carmen asked for a couple of days to digest the request and had plans to discuss with Professor Scaffale. She may not have known exactly what the solution would be, but she did know that this was not Mrs. Moore's responsibility, it was her own.

Professor Scaffale was unavailable in person, so they arranged to speak by phone. Carmen passed along Sally's story with every emotional detail. She expressed how frustrated Sally was the best that she could describe and waited patiently for an answer. Dr. Scaffale responded, "You've already read the answer to this dilemma in one of our previous book studies, Learning by Doing. Since you were more focused on the PLC parts of the book, we never really discussed the chapter focused on administrators. Go back and re-read it and call me back tomorrow afternoon."

Carmen didn't need to reread the chapter. She knew exactly what Professor Scaffale was talking about, but she needed time to mull it over anyhow. What he was talking about was Richard DuFour's idea that administrators should be bottom up when possible and top down when necessary. She preferred the idea that he once wrote in a paper that if you want to make diamonds, you need pressure from above and support from below. One without the other is insufficient.

Carmen was pretty good at the support part, but hadn't had much practice with the pressure part. It appeared that it may now be time for some pressure.

She wasn't excited about this part as her approach to confrontation was to avoid it at all cost. And sometimes, like in this case, that cost was heavy.

When Dr. Esposito called Dr. Scaffale back the next day, they discussed how to put this idea into practice. He echoed the ideas of DuFour's article that "top down" doesn't mean the same thing as "heavy-handed." Top-down leadership can be done with compassion without harming relationships. Top down can simply mean being very clear about expectations, deciding what it will look like when those expectations are met, and what support will be given if expectations are not met.

Carmen agreed that she had not done a very good job with the top down part of the equation and although she was clear inside her head what her own expectations are, she had never explained them clearly to others. Carmen had spent years on bottom up and didn't regret a moment of it, but this was a case where top down would be the correct approach. But, it is going to have to be a delicate dance to preserve relationships, especially the relationship with Sally Moore through this situation.

"But," she complained, "DuFour's article isn't very practical. I completely agree with his argument, but I still don't know how to do it." Professor Scaffale got that look on his face again and he asked, "What do you think about the Wizard of Oz?" It appeared that Scaffale had upgraded to a tablet now and he tapped away at the screen with one finger and then flipped the screen around. *How Did That Happen?* showed on the screen and Carmen knew what was in store, another long night of reading.

Dr. Scaffale handed her the tablet and said, "Here, I got this for you so that you don't have to wait for your books to come in the mail anymore. In 3 seconds, that book will be finished downloading. Two, One, done!" Carmen took a deep, nervous breath fearing that she would be up late reading about things that she would be uncomfortable putting into practice.

Again, when Professor Scaffale came back the following week, there were posters all over the walls with scribbles, words, and pictures. What he could read right away on the top of the posters was, "Form Expectations: Non-negotiables," "Communicate Expectations: Manifesto," "Align Expectations: Leadership Team," and "Inspect Expectations: Learning Walks."

The professor could once again see that Carmen had processed the book and turned it into an action plan. In a short 73 minutes, she had explained the whole thing to him whizzing from poster to poster excitedly. *How Did That Happen* had helped Carmen realize that she had really let her expectations falter for some time now. She had not addressed the non-negotiables in at least four faculty meetings. The manifesto had begun collecting dust on a shelf. The social studies department had forgotten all about the meetings norms they had created and their meetings had begun to deteriorate again.

Carmen knew exactly what she had to do. She needed to clarify her expectations of the social studies department and all other departments for that matter. She also needed to reassess progress toward the goals in the manifesto. She immediately added non-negotiables to the next meeting agenda. She also decided that she would be present at the next social studies department meeting to ensure that norms were being followed and expectations were being met.

Carmen was satisfied that she found a solution that was top down, but not heavy-handed. If this plan did not work, she may have to be a little more heavy-handed. But at this point, the plan for moving forward was respectful, top-down intervention with clear expectations at the forefront.

LEADERSHIP REFERENCE: *HOW DID THAT HAPPEN?* AND *WHAT GREAT PRINCIPALS DO DIFFERENTLY*

The subtitle of Connors and Smith's *How Did That Happen?* was exactly what Carmen was looking for, "Holding people accountable for results the positive, principled way" and was the follow-up to their book, *The Oz Principle: Getting Results through Individual and Organizational Accountability.*

The Oz Principle uses characters from the Wizard of Oz to teach about personal and organizational accountability. The authors use the phrase "above the line" to mean meeting organizational expectations and "below the line" for excuses and cover-ups for not meeting expectations. *How Did That Happen* focuses solely on the expectations part of that equation. The book promotes the idea that when an employee does not meet an expectation, the leader should first reflect and ask, "How did I allow that to happen?" One major reason that an employee does not meet expectations is that the expectations were not clear.

One example from the author's experience came while sitting in the classroom of a new teacher who wanted the rest of the class to see one student's excellent work. As such, she said, "I'd like you all to come up and see this work." Students got up and began wandering around the room looking for good work. The teacher got very upset with the students. Students wandered around the room because they did not understand what the teacher was asking them to do and did the best that they could. Instead, she should have said, "There is some excellent work up here on the front table. When I call out the number of your row, I would like you to each stand up, push in your chair, and quietly walk up here to see it." That method explains her expectations clearly, reduces confusion, and gives students a path to meet her expectations.

Chapter 15 also referenced *What Great Principals Do Differently: Fifteen Things That Matter Most* by Todd Whitaker. Todd's book is a series of stories demonstrating important factors in being a great principal. Most of the factors are related to building good relationships, communicating well, not holding back high achievers, and setting strong expectations.

What Great Principals Do Differently deals with topics such as basing your decisions on your best teachers, not your worst teachers; treat everyone with respect; and it's about the people, not the programs. These are typical topics for an educational leadership book, but the stories that go along with each really drive the recommendations home and make them memorable and applicable.

REFLECTION QUESTIONS

1. What flawed strategies are being used at your school and being justified with flawed logic? What can you do to change this?
2. What are you doing to teach your leaders how to lead? What could you do better in this area?
3. In what areas could you be better at explaining your expectations to your followers? How would you know when you have become successful at this task?

Chapter 16

Perfect Practice

Will we be content to cruise along on autopilot or will we scramble and suffer to get better?

—Doug Lemov

"I had been riding on a high for months thinking that I was an amazing leader because I had given others some leadership responsibility. But there are some leadership responsibilities that remain with those at the top. This was one of those times and I realized that I had been negligent in my duties because, for the most part, things had been running pretty smoothly.

I hurt great friends like Mrs. Moore in the process by making them bear burdens that did not belong on their shoulders. I was the epitome of 'Good is the enemy of great.' Things were going well, so I sat back a little and let the status quo run its course. The status quo at this point in time was good, maybe very good, but it wasn't perfect."

Carmen wished deeply that Mrs. Moore could have attended her retirement party so that she could apologize for the thousandth time, but she also understood the passion for the work that she was doing in Tanzania. Carmen contributed books to the project whenever she could and always planned to visit, but never had. Now that she is retired, maybe she will have time to reconnect with one of her oldest friends, one who she still feels guilty about how things turned out at times.

Carmen had just read several books that praised the practice of practice. It started with *Outliers* and the 10,000 hour rule. This made her wonder how talent played into expertise. The author, Malcolm Gladwell, said that there is no such thing as talent. There are those who have put in 10,000 hours of deliberate practice and those who have not. So, Carmen read "Talent is Overrated" and "The Talent Myth" that supported this idea but only gave examples of musicians and athletes.

She wondered how a principal can deliberately practice the art and science of administration. The answer came in another book, one that she had discovered on her own through the e-book reader that Dr. Scaffale had given her. It was called *Practice Perfect* and almost all of the examples were related to education. It answered all of the questions she was left with after binge reading books about talent and practice in other fields for weeks.

After delving into all of this reading about talent, Carmen found that the one thing all of the books had in common was that they agreed that becoming an expert requires deliberate, precise practice under conditions as similar as possible to the real situation. *Practice Perfect* recommended that administrators practice difficult conversations with colleagues and that teachers practice new strategies in department meetings. Carmen realized that her next step was to have a partner act out the part of the other person while she practiced these difficult conversations.

Carmen practiced and practiced with her boyfriend and Mrs. Toms. She rehearsed the conversation in her mind while driving, but she still was not ready. She continued scripting, practicing in front of the mirror, rehearsing with colleagues, and pondering while at the gym. She followed a script that she learned in the "InsideOut Coaching" training and still did not feel completely comfortable, like she might be blindsided by a pointed question.

This is why Carmen preferred email over face-to-face at times. She could write, rewrite, edit, research, and rewrite again. It still felt like something was missing from her practice; like she was prepared to say the right things but that there must be something more to it.

Carmen called Professor Scaffale and explained her predicament to him. He was highly impressed by the work that she had put in so far and suspected that he had an idea what was missing. It would be so unlike him to just tell her, so instead, he recommended another book. This one was called *Crucial Conversations* and Carmen asked herself, "Why have I never heard of this book before? The title sounds perfect!"

LEADERSHIP REFERENCE: *PRACTICE PERFECT*

Practice Perfect by Doug Lemov first points out that just doing a task over and over is not deliberate practice. A principal cannot say, "I have made 12 phone calls today, I have practiced my communication skills." The practice that Lemov discusses is much more fine-grained and deliberate than that. He argues that one must practice each skill broken down into small pieces in as close to a real world setting as possible.

For example, instead of practicing phone calls, Carmen might practice speaking tentatively (a *Crucial Conversations* strategy that will be discussed in the next chapter) while on the phone. She would have a mentor sitting with her while she is practicing this skill and giving her feedback on how she did. This is the kind of deliberate practice with immediate feedback that Lemov is referring to.

Teachers can practice this in department meetings with other teachers as stand-ins for students. Principals can practice this way with a mentor and colleagues as support and actors. The book gives many examples of how teachers and administrators can practice getting better at the art and science of education and leadership.

REFLECTION QUESTIONS

1. How do you decide which actions will be top-down and which will be bottom up? Are you happy with your ratio of the two?
2. How do you deliberately practice being a better leader? How do you give teachers an opportunity to practice?
3. Which parts of leadership do you try to avoid (conflict, politics, crucial conversations)? How could you use deliberate practice to get better at these things?

Chapter 17

Thank You

A word fitly spoken is like apples of gold in baskets of silver.

—Kerry Patterson

"I learned a great deal from Crucial Conversations and it changed me both personally and professionally. I was doing many things wrong in my conversations and I had a great deal of learning and practice to work on. What I discovered was missing from my plan for this particular conversation was safety. I don't mean that I was going to take self-defense lessons, but I needed to create a safe environment for an honest discussion before having these difficult conversations. If the other person doesn't feel safe, then they'll get defensive and everything falls apart."

"I had been getting along depending on relationships to prevent difficult conversations, but that can only take a leader so far. Eventually, creating the safety to have a crucial conversation is unavoidable. This skill set has proven beneficial in all aspects of my life. It's not magical, but without safety, your carefully selected words don't matter. It turns out that even with safety and lots and lots of practice, that meeting didn't go how I had hoped. Two of the social studies teachers transferred at the end of the year and it almost launched me into another fit of depression."

Carmen realized that she was on a soap box and decided that it was probably time to fast-forward the story.

When she got back to her office after the meeting with the social studies department, Carmen went through cycles of emotions—rage, disappointment, sadness, fear, and then back to rage again. She had done everything right and still the meeting failed miserably. She was going through the entire conversation word by word in her mind and couldn't figure out where she went wrong.

Carmen had reflected during the conversation to analyze the safety in the room. She kept self-monitoring her "silence or violence" levels. She paraphrased and asked questions. She explained her purpose for the meeting and gave background information to explain her "story." She felt like she had done everything just as the book had said. Maybe the book was wrong.

Just then, she was pulled back to reality when a familiar voice said, "You can't win them all. I told you that it was a tough crowd." It was Sally. They sat there after school had let out and vented for almost 2 hours going back and forth telling stories and reassuring each other. Carmen walked through the entire *Crucial Conversations* playbook, even taking out a legal pad to diagram out some of the mnemonics from the book and how she had infused them into the conversation.

"I started with heart, created synergy, told my stories, I talked tentatively, and I monitored for silence or violence. I don't know where I went wrong." Carmen stopped talking about the book long enough to again apologize to Mrs. Moore for putting her into this situation for so long. One meeting with the department and Carmen was drained. She can't even imagine how Sally must feel doing this every week.

Carmen put her forehead in the palm of her hand and let out a frustrated sigh as the conversation was wrapping up. She said to Sally, "I thought I'd come so far. Was it all just a façade and nothing has really changed?" She wasn't borderline depressed anymore, she was depressed and that was never good for herself or anyone around her.

Sally got out of her chair and began to walk over to Carmen's desk. "May I do something on your computer?" she asked. She took Carmen's mouse and pulled up the inbox on her email. "One, two . . . three . . . yeah, four, five . . . six, seven, good one, eight," she counted slowly.

"What are you doing?" Carmen requested.

"I'm counting how many thank-you emails you've received today. You're worried about one or two people who don't belong to your fan club, but you had at least 9 emails today thanking you for something great that you did for someone else. THIS is how you should be measuring your success, the number of thank-you messages that you have in your inbox and on your voicemail every day.

You told us two years ago that your leadership style is 'Servant Leadership' but I think that it's more 'Family Leadership.' You lead us by loving us and doing favors for us, feeding us and being interested in our lives, knowing our children's names and always having our backs with parents, protecting us from the ivory tower and going out of your way to remove barriers. You've helped us become a family. It just happens that one branch of the family tree is weak right now. But don't forget that there are dozens of other branches that are strong. And they're strong because of your support and your leadership. And we are thankful for that."

"Here is the perfect example I was looking for. I'm going to copy and paste this one for you and hang it above your computer for you to see every day." After some typing, printer whirring, and scissors cutting, Sally pulled off two pieces of transparent tape and stuck a small paper to the wall. Carmen walked over to see what it said.

She read aloud, "Thank you. I should never have doubted you. I know that you ALWAYS have our backs." Carmen remembered this email coming from a teacher who had asked for a favor and checked back regularly, almost to the point of being annoying, to make sure that it had been taken care of. Carmen took pride in following through on her promises and Sally was right that this was further reassurance that her teachers had noticed her efforts and trusted her deeply.

By this time, Carmen was so full of mixed emotions that she couldn't even speak. As she walked with Sally toward the door, all that she could eek out is, "I'm the one who owes you a thank you." Sally smiled and said, "That's one for me," and made an imaginary tick mark in the air with her finger.

LEADERSHIP REFERENCE: *CRUCIAL CONVERSATIONS*

Kerry Patterson and Joseph Grenny's *Crucial Conversations* is best summarized by its subtitle, "Tools for Talking When Stakes Are High." The book lays out a game plan for having difficult conversations from asking for a raise to discussing the details of a divorce settlement, from disciplining an employee to negotiating a contract.

One of the key aspects of the book is to ensure that there is an environment of safety, one in which people feel free to speak openly, before beginning a crucial conversation. The authors also advocate sharing stories, but not how one might think. Two people can look at exactly the same evidence and come to two different conclusions because the different life experiences they have lived through have led them to different inner stories which lead to different conclusions. Sharing one's inner story and asking to hear another's story leads to a greater probability of agreement or at least mutual understanding.

Crucial Conversations constantly refers back to the "silence or violence" response that many people have in these situations and how a leader can effectively deal with these innate reactions. Developing mutual purpose, showing genuine interest, and asking probing questions can help to surpass a silence or violence barrier. One of the most valuable lessons in the book is, when someone says something that seems particularly unprofessional or uncharacteristic, a leader should reflect on the question, "Why would a reasonable, rational, and decent person do this?" This switches the conversation back to empathy and respect which leads to safety.

REFLECTION QUESTIONS

1. How do you encourage your teachers to "share their stories" or explain the logic behind their conclusions?
2. How do you create safety before an important conversation? What crucial conversations are you avoiding because safety has not been established?
3. How do you measure your success as a leader?

Chapter 18

Vital Behaviors

When dealing with people, remember you are not dealing with creatures of logic, but creatures of emotion.

—Dale Carnegie

Dr. Esposito looked out at the crowd and did not see the two social studies teachers who left that year sitting in the crowd. She invited them, but wasn't holding her breath as their relationship was cordial, but not friendly. To this day, she still had not been able to let this perceived failure go. It haunted her for many years and after many attempts, she was never able to have proper crucial conversations with the social studies department. She had allowed too much bad blood to develop before facing the beast head on.

"Thanks to Sally, I became obsessed with counting how many times people thanked me in a day. It really changed my outlook on the job and made me a better servant leader. The last quarter of that year alone, I received 297 thank you messages. It made me feel good and like I was accomplishing something, but it didn't fix my relationship with the social studies department. I also became better at saying thank you to others."

"I would highly recommend that leaders in this room also count acts of thanks and increase how often you say thank you. It changed the way I think and the way that I lead. I still feel proud every time someone says thank you to me." At that moment, Mrs. Toms looked up from the front table and mouthed "Thank you" silently to Carmen.

"My relationship with all of the other departments was very good, I was facing difficult conversations head on, but I still couldn't let this one department go. Over the next several weeks, I tried again and again to make a breakthrough and I could not get through to them. My tribe leaders tried and failed also."

"I then became obsessed with reading about leadership, influence, and motivation. I read at least ten more books, attended conferences, watched TED videos. In the end, the book that helped me to connect with this department and other departments better was more than 70 years old."

Carmen tried not to call Professor Scaffale on this one to see if she had learned enough to handle the situation on her own. The leadership team had really learned to love Daniel Pink as an author and in the present situation they had discussed a book called *To Sell Is Human*. The foreign language department chair told her that the gist of the book is that all of life is sales and all of sales is influence. We sell interviewers that we are the best candidate, we sell foundations that we are deserving of grants, we sell the board of education that we are educating children well, and we sell students that we have put them in the proper courses.

Of course, this focus on influence led her to read a book entitled *Influencer: The Power to Change Anything*. This book had a great deal of practical advice in it that would guide her interactions with teachers in the school. It worked perfectly with autonomy, mastery, and purpose; in that, it suggests figuring out what the two or three vital behaviors are absolutely necessary to be good at something and focusing diligently on those.

Part of the process of determining those vital behaviors is to study positive deviance sometimes through vicarious experiences and that's exactly what was happening in the learning walks. She felt like she was already doing so much of the work that Patterson and the other authors were recommending. It was relieving.

Finally, Carmen couldn't help it any longer and called Professor Scaffale. When she told him about the two books that she had read in his absence he responded, "Those are two of my favorites! If you like those, you'll love Dale Carnegie." Those words would literally change everything, again. The book Dr. Scaffale was referring to was *How to Win Friends and Influence People*. This book was written by Dale Carnegie in 1936 and had been republished several times, selling more than 15 million copies. Dr. Scaffale brought her a copy of the book that was so worn that she wondered if it might be an actual 1936 copy.

When the professor returned to discuss the book, he once again noticed posters all over her walls. He commented, "Wow, you really love posters. Let's see, what do we have here?" As he looked around, he saw one poster with large writing and small notes all over it. The large writing said,

How to Handle People
Don't criticize, condemn or complain.
Give honest and sincere appreciation.
Arouse in the other person an eager want.

He noticed that the small writing was her notes for how she might put these principles into practice. As he began to read the small writing, Carmen joked, "If I'd read this book in college, I would have been a better wife, a better mother, a better student, a better teacher, and certainly a better leader. It is just full of gems."

As Professor Scaffale rotated around, he saw another poster that read:

Six ways to make people like you

1. Become genuinely interested in other people.
2. Smile.
3. Remember that a person's name is to that person the sweetest and most important sound in any language.
4. Be a good listener. Encourage others to talk about themselves.
5. Talk in terms of the other person's interests.
6. Make the other person feel important—and do it sincerely.

The professor noticed that number 5 was circled multiple times and he commented, "It looks like number 5 is very important to you. Why is that?" Carmen appreciated how Dr. Scaffale had just focused the conversation on what was important to her, just like Dale Carnegie would have recommended. He chose to ask the question this way instead of something like, "I'm curious, why is number 5 so important to you? I prefer number 3," and making the question about his own curiosity and preferences.

Carmen explained that she had realized that many of her issues with the social studies department could have been prevented if she hadn't focused on what was in it for her, but rather what was in it for the teachers. She gave him an example,

"When we were searching for a new book for the department, I argued that it would make me look cooperative with district administrators if we selected the same book as the other two high schools in the district. What a self-centered idiot that must have made me look like.

What I should have argued is that if we selected the same book as the other schools, their fruitless curriculum meetings would be more productive, it would be easier to write common assessments, pacing would be similar so transfer students could jump right in, new teachers would be easily supported, and the shared network drive could finally be used to share lesson plans between sites as it was intended. Teachers would save time writing lessons and rubrics and could focus more on the enjoyable parts of teaching." Scaffale grinned with an expression of pride in how much Carmen had already learned about Carnegie's philosophies.

There were several other posters, but one stood out that had writing all over it in different penmanship and different colors. "That one, we discussed at our last Leadership Team meeting," Carmen explained. It read:

Change People without Giving Offense or Arousing Resentment

1. Begin with praise and honest appreciation.
2. Call attention to people's mistakes indirectly.
3. Talk about your own mistakes before criticizing the other person.
4. Ask questions instead of giving direct orders.
5. Let the other person save face.
6. Praise the slightest improvement and praise every improvement.
7. Give the other person a fine reputation to live up to.
8. Use encouragement. Make the fault seem easy to correct.
9. Make the other person happy about doing the thing you suggest.

One thing that the professor noticed written numerous times on the poster in multiple different colors was "ESTD." He asked about the meaning and Carmen blushed with embarrassment a little as she responded, "Easier said than done." Professor Scaffale reassured her that the team is absolutely correct and that theoretical leadership research is always much easier than the everyday implementation of the findings, but no leadership author would ever admit that. Creating a safe environment, admitting that you're wrong, and holding adults accountable for moving the vision along are all easier to write about than they are to actually implement.

LEADERSHIP REFERENCE: *HOW TO WIN FRIENDS AND INFLUENCE PEOPLE*

Dale Carnegie's *How to Win Friends and Influence People* is on almost every list of the best leadership books of all times. Carnegie presents lists of suggestions for handling people, making people like you, winning people over to your way of thinking, and on being a leader. The lists are practical and supported with stories, research, and Carnegie's experience with some of the most famous leaders in history.

All of Carnegie's lists are built around integrity, relationship building, honesty, empathy, and listening. The topics include "Fundamental Techniques in Handling People," "Six Ways to Make People Like You," "How to Win People to Your Way of Thinking," and "Be a Leader." Some of the topics sound politically incorrect through a twenty-first-century lens, but the pages are filled with positivity and excellent advice.

REFLECTION QUESTIONS

1. If you could narrow great teaching down to three vital behaviors, which would they be?
2. How good are you at avoiding criticism and complaining? What could you do to be better at this? What are your triggers?
3. How can you reframe your conversations with your followers to focus on the other person's interests?

Chapter 19

Love and Trust

Whether you're on a sports team, in an office or a member of a family, if you can't trust one another there's going to be trouble.

—Stephen M. R. Covey

Those Dale Carnegie posters had been so important in Dr. Esposito's personal and professional lives that she still has them. As she unrolled one of the posters on the stage and held it in front of her face to hide the tears that were beginning to flow again, she said, "One thing that Dale forgot is that the final rule of leadership should be, 'Don't talk too long when you have a captive audience.'" The audience knew exactly what she was trying to say, but they also did not want the speech to end. The end of the speech would signal the end of her career to those sitting in this room. Many of them could not bear this thought.

"As I look around this room, I don't see colleagues or co-workers, I see great friends and close family. When I realized in the middle of my career that the best schools were those in which the faculty felt like family, I never considered that it works both ways. Not only did I see all of you connect with each other, but I grew to love every single one of you. I thought that I would set up a situation where you would all love each other like family, but I ended up loving you all like family as well." The room burst into laughter again when one of the social studies teachers in the back yelled out, "Even me?" Carmen smiled and replied, "Especially you."

"I won't hold you any longer, I just want to leave you with one last thought. Many of you know that I never really recovered from my divorce or the death of my mother. Even after I met the man of my dreams who I plan to spend the rest of my life with, I was still lonely and I buried myself in books. I struggled with depression for years and it took me a long time to find a combination of medication and therapy that allowed me to perform at a strong level."

"In fact, Dr. Scaffale doesn't even really exist. He is just the name that I have for the conversations in my head about the hundreds of books that I buried myself in to escape it all. When I was a child, I was full of questions, much like I am now. Whenever I asked my grandmother one of my crazy questions, 'Why do worms come out when it rains?', 'What would my fingers look like if I sat in the bathtub for a week?', or 'Can you teach goldfish to do tricks?', she always had the same answer, 'Go ask Professor Scaffale.' In Italian, 'scaffale' means bookshelf and it was her grandmotherly way to tell me to go look it up myself or to go to the library. She must have told me that ten thousand times which is probably why I still love books so much even today."

"This leads me right into my final announcement, my husband and I are moving to Italy in a few months where I plan to relax all day and have conversations with Dr. Scaffale about sordid romance novels, classic literature, and tabloids. I'll sit by the pool, sip Sangria, and visit the library where my grandmother and I used to talk to Dr. Scaffale."

"I hope that Professor Scaffale and I have added something valuable to your life and have enriched you in some way. If I can summarize in one sentence everything I've learned from the good doctor, I'd have to say that trust, two-way, mutual, unconditional trust is more important to the success of a school or a life than anything else."

She added, while winking at the table with the redwood tree, "Our leadership team knows that building trust is ESTD, so they decided to put another book in all of your gift bags that we all found very useful, *The Speed of Trust* which will walk you gently through the process of building trust with your colleagues. I want to thank you all . . . thank you . . . I'm sorry."

Carmen walked back to her chair unable to speak anymore. A mixture of tears and laughter passed through the room as everyone began to consider the idea of going back to the school and not seeing Carmen there anymore. If Carmen was uncomfortable speaking in front of people, she was really going to be uncomfortable with what was to come next.

Carmen's thoughts went back to one of the leadership meetings which now had a regular agenda item, "What are we going to do about the social studies team?" This had been on the agenda for at least two years and little progress had been made. One of the assistant superintendents had decided to sit in on this meeting and Carmen could still remember the looks on the team's faces when he said, "It sounds like they don't trust you guys."

At once, the whole team sighed with a, "Why didn't we think about that?" kind of exasperation. There had been such a strained relationship with this department for so long that they distrusted the entire leadership team, Carmen, and the entire district office. Without fixing that, nothing would get better. Hopefully, *The Speed of Trust* would provide some answers as they read it together as a team.

At the next meeting, the assistant superintendent volunteered to come back and lead a discussion about his favorite book with the team. Carmen sat back and just listened as they discussed ideas for how to learn to trust themselves and how to build trust with the social studies department. Nobody had any idea what she was contemplating. They discussed at length how the keys to trusting oneself were to develop integrity, intent, capabilities, and results. It struck them quickly how well these four factors aligned with the other books that they had read together.

They remembered the golden rule, "Live a life of undivided integrity." They discussed how "capabilities" and "mastery" were so similar. These similarities helped them to feel like this was not a brand new venture, but something they already had experience with. The assistant superintendent explained that this was also a very important lesson in leadership, to frame change as simply slight modifications of what we are already doing. They began to discuss relational trust and organizational trust when something did not feel right. The assistant superintendent was still speaking, but most of the room had stopped paying attention a few minutes ago.

The team suddenly realized that Carmen had not spoken in some time now and they all turned to her at once. They were shocked to see that her eyes were glassy and they rushed over to ensure that she was ok. "I have something to tell you and I don't know how, so I'm just going to say it. The end of this school year will be my last. I'm retiring." Suddenly, all of the eyes in the room went glassy. The assistant superintendent must have told someone at the district office because Carmen got at least ten voicemails that night. She ignored them all. She just could not handle it right now.

LEADERSHIP REFERENCE: *THE SPEED OF TRUST*

The Speed of Trust by Stephen M. R. Covey can best be summarized by a quote from the book, "There is one thing that is common to every individual, relationship, team, family, organization, nation, economy, and civilization throughout the world—one thing which, if removed, will destroy the most powerful government, the most successful business, the most thriving economy, the most influential leadership, the greatest friendship, the strongest character, the deepest love.

On the other hand, if developed and leveraged, that one thing has the potential to create unparalleled success and prosperity in every dimension of life. Yet, it is the least understood, most neglected, and most underestimated possibility of our time. That one thing is trust."

The Speed of Trust discusses thoroughly the importance of two-way trust. Covey talks about five waves of trust, but really only the first three apply to schools, self-trust, relationship trust, and organizational trust. There are some commonalities between the waves like integrity, honesty, and transparency. There are some very important lessons about trust for leaders within the pages, for example, how difficult it is to build trust and how easy it is to destroy it.

REFLECTION QUESTIONS

1. How does your integrity contribute to your self-trust? What can you do to increase your self-trust?
2. What capabilities do you lack that devalue your self-trust? How can you improve in these areas?
3. How close are you to achieving organizational trust? Who in the organization is missing? What can you do in order for everyone to trust each other?

Chapter 20

El Niño

Listening, coupled with regular periods of reflection, are essential to the growth of the servant-leader.

—Robert K. Greenleaf

The retired superintendent walked back to the microphone obviously emotional and clearly with tears on her cheeks and puffy eyes. "Now, I'd like to invite some of Carmen's 'best friends' to come up and share some of their favorite stories about her leadership. I know that everyone would love to come up and speak about some of the amazing interactions they've had. But to get out of here at a reasonable time, we've scheduled a handful of people to speak, we'll have some open mic for a few others to speak, and then Carmen will stick around to chat."

Carmen slowly shook her head but knew that she could neither escape nor do anything to stop this. In planning this event, she fought the idea of having friends come up and speak about her, but she lost the battle and would now have to squirm in her chair as the memories flowed. Carmen was the type who would cry at a funeral not for the deceased, but for the grief of the families they left behind. She could not bear the idea of sitting there listening to people mourn her in her retirement.

The superintendent glanced at Carmen with a sly smile and said, "First up is Mr. Baker from the social studies department." Carmen's face popped up from her hands in surprise. Mr. Baker was not her biggest fan the first five or six years working together. She had not even noticed that Mr. Baker was in the crowd, that was probably by design in retrospect. Now, she could see him, sitting low in a beanbag chair hiding behind the group of social studies teachers in the back of the room.

Chapter 20

Mr. Baker respectfully set down his clipboard and giant red pen before walking up the stairs to the stage. He made eye contact with Carmen and tried to reassure her with a smile, but it was clear that she was still afraid to hear what he was going to say. The two had a history of public email battles and an occasional argument or two during a faculty meeting. They were heated, but never unprofessional.

Mr. Baker began, "It was no secret that the social studies department as a whole and myself as an individual were not very welcoming when Carmen first took over as principal. We had decided that since the chances were good that she wouldn't last more than a few months, we shouldn't put much effort into getting to know her. Every month at our department meeting, we would begin with the 'Can you believe that she's still here?' commentary."

"After two years, we were baffled that she hadn't taken a job at an easier school or at the district office. And then at about the 4 year mark, she won my heart. It wasn't the effort that she put into her faculty meetings, it wasn't how she tried to protect us from politics and bureaucracy, it wasn't even the snacks that she always had in her office . . . although that WAS pretty good."

"See, there was one evening during an unusually wet El Niño winter that a huge storm hit the school. We must have gotten 4 inches of rain in one night! Everyone here knows how well the drains in the quad work when the fuzz from the artificial grass clogs them. The drains clogged with fuzz and leaves and the water pooled up finding its way right up to my classroom door as it always had for years before Carmen. Within minutes, it would be flooding my entire classroom."

"When I arrived at school the next morning, I was in a horrible mood. I was sure that I would have to move to another classroom while they dried the carpet and removed the mold. An entire stack of interactive notebooks would be ruined. The classroom would smell horrible. It would be weeks of mayhem before this was fixed."

"Then as I walked out of the office to yell at someone, what did I see? I saw a figure standing in the middle of the pond of water in a business suit with the legs rolled up, water above her ankles, and clearing the drains in the quad with a big push broom. Occasionally, she bent over and grabbed a handful of . . . muck out of the drain. It was Carmen! It was clear that she had been there for several hours, probably arriving at 4 in the morning. She was shivering cold, wet up to the knees, with two handfuls of disgusting muck."

"At that moment, I realized that all of her attempts at winning us over were genuine. She wasn't just using the school as a stepping stone. She really cared about us. Her work in the quad early that morning saved my classroom and the three classrooms around me from water damage. I stood there and marveled for at least 5 minutes. She was working so hard to protect us that she didn't even notice me there and the look of awe that must have been on my face."

Mr. Baker pulled the microphone out of the stand and turned to Carmen and said, "Carmen, I believe that a true leader is not one who pulls followers from the front, but one who rolls up her pant legs and pushes from behind then walks alongside. Thank you for leading us."

As she got over the shock and hugged Mr. Baker, Carmen reflected on that cold, wet day. She had become obsessed with leadership books. When she saw a book called *Servant Leadership* by Robert Greenleaf at the bookstore, she was intrigued. She carried it around in the bookstore for a while debating whether she had time to be a servant or not. She ended up being enormously pleased that she purchased the book that day.

After reading the book, she was dedicated to serving more and micromanaging less. But servant leadership, she found, is not a list of tasks, skills, or behaviors. Instead, it is a way of thinking and ways of thinking take time to change. Carmen found herself repeatedly disappointed because after the fact, she would realize that she had just missed an opportunity to serve. She had opportunities to help others grow but instead told them what to do or how to do it.

She started small. Instead of saying "I don't know," she started saying, "Let's learn about this together." It was not a huge change in the beginning, but it was a shift from putting the responsibility on the other individual to taking responsibility herself to help the other person grow. Not everyone liked it in the beginning and if she had not built trust first, some may have seen it as a sign that she did not know the answers.

Carmen moved up to bigger things as her mindset started changing. When she hired a new teacher the day before school began, the teacher came to visit the empty, dull classroom and they realized simultaneously that all of the furniture was still in boxes stacked in the corner. Carmen stayed until 3:00 a.m. and set off the alarm twice putting that furniture together with that new teacher. They talked about so many things. Carmen learned about her dreams and ambitions and was able to serve her better and help her grow as a result.

It felt so good that Carmen ended up building three desks, five bookshelves, and nine filing cabinets that week while speaking with teachers. She even learned what a "tamper-proof torx bit" was when mounting a projector for one of the social studies teachers. She got to know the teacher, who now trusted and respected her and put a deposit in her emotional bank account.

But Carmen also realized that servant leadership is not just about physically serving the faculty. It is also about helping the faculty accomplish their dreams and become leaders themselves. This was the realization that led to the learning walks, the leadership team, and partnering with the university to get cohorts of student teachers at the school. Many of those student teachers ended up working at the school and becoming some of the best teachers the school had ever seen.

After several years of increased servant leadership, Carmen realized that her thoughts were changing and she really was becoming a servant leader. Her thoughts had changed from "How can I lead you, convince you, and change you?" to "How can I help you be a better teacher and a better leader?" That was when she knew that the transformation to servant leader was complete.

LEADERSHIP REFERENCE: *SERVANT LEADERSHIP*

Servant Leadership: A Journey into the Nature of Legitimate Power & Greatness by Robert Greenleaf was originally written in 1977 and has been updated numerous times. The messages in the book align with many other leadership books, notably that a leader must have integrity, empathy, and vision, as well as being someone that others will want to follow. Greenleaf spends a great deal of time describing the strong trust that must exist between a servant leader and their followers. He proposes that the greatest test of whether a leader is a servant or not is if their followers become more autonomous as they follow. Carmen would certainly agree with that.

Greenleaf was one of the first to define manager versus leader in this book and proposes that personal effort should be given to leading processes instead of being administrator of day-to-day operations. He condones a credit-giving, nearly invisible leader whose faith in the mission is unwavering. The bottom line of the book is that the leader's main job is not the corporate mission, but to guide the people within the corporation. A leader must insure that their follower's highest priority needs are being met. When she first began, their basic needs were not even being met.

Greenleaf proposes that the best test for being a successful servant leader is whether those who follow you grow as a person. Carmen looked around this room filled with colleagues, leaders, and followers and knew absolutely that she had been successful in this mission.

REFLECTION QUESTIONS

1. How do you develop the leadership skills of your followers? How do you assist aspiring administrators to improve their skills?
2. A servant leader decides to serve first and that service develops into a desire to lead. What opportunities do your aspiring leaders have to serve others?
3. Servant leaders share power with those around them. How do you share your power with others?

Chapter 21

The Surprise

Adults need to come to understand that the child does not want any of our power. He merely wants some of his own.

—Richard Lavoie

Mr. Baker thanked the audience, hugged Carmen again, and announced that he was going to begin working on his master's degree and administrative credential. He told the emotional audience that he was going to pass the microphone along before he began to cry himself. "Next up," he said, "is Sally Moore."

Shocked faces began scanning the room. Sally had just landed at the airport from Tanzania 2 hours ago and grabbed a rideshare straight here. This is why Dr. Vasquez had left the room for a few minutes, to set up the surprise. Carmen should have known that Sally would not have missed this event for the world. She and Carmen loved to surprise each other and this was a big one. They had a history of birthday surprises so grand that many had suggested that they start a video blog channel about their adventures.

This was particularly surprising to Carmen because Sally never wanted to be the center of attention either. She rarely said more than a few sentences in a leadership team meeting. Sally fumbled with her papers on the podium clearly trying to get over some nervous energy on top of the adrenaline from rushing from the airport. She took a rubber band off of a long tube of paper and unrolled a poster. When she opened it up, the audience could see that it was a poster that the whole school was familiar with, "Excellence: Every Classroom, Every Lesson, Every Day." They had all seen it a million times.

Sally began, "I have a story similar to Mr. Baker's. There was one single event that finally showed me that Carmen was not in this for fame, glory, or a promotion. We were in a leadership meeting once and we were brainstorming ideas. To everyone's surprise, I spoke up and came up with the phrase, 'Excellence: Every Classroom, Every Lesson, Every Day.' We made notepads, bumper stickers, door mats, and posters." At that point, she held the poster up high. "It's not the posters or the bumper stickers that impressed me. What impressed me is what is at the bottom of each poster and bumper sticker."

The audience seemed confused. Sally held up the poster and pointed to a line of text at the bottom that read, "—Sally Moore." The audience began to understand. "There were only five people in the room at the time that this phrase was invented. I thought for sure . . . no, I knew . . . that Carmen was going to take credit for the idea. All principals do that, right? They take credit for the test scores that the teachers accomplish. They take credit for the clean campus that the custodians create. They even take credit for football victories that they really have nothing to do with. But, as I would learn, Carmen is not like this."

At this point, the audience had pulled out the bumper stickers from their gift bags sitting on the table. They had not noticed the attribution at the bottom before and smiled as they saw it now. "I know that it sounds self-centered of me, but I was very proud of that phrase and I couldn't sleep or eat, consumed with the dreadful idea that Carmen was going to take credit. So, when she brought copies of the notepads to the next leadership meeting with my name on it, I was sold."

"She was not the typical administrator that I had seen time after time in my career. She had integrity and hope. After that, Carmen earned an advocate in me. She has done a million things to help us and to help the students at our school. But that one act is what convinced me once and for all that everything that Carmen did was for our benefit and the benefit of our students, not for her own benefit. Carmen finally made me feel like a professional. Thank you, Carmen." The two introverts hugged each other with a nod acknowledging the uncomfortable feeling of being up on stage.

Carmen remembered this situation well. This was in her "good to great" phase and she really took to heart the idea that a Level 5 leader gives credit and takes blame. She was extremely proud of Sally at that meeting and went on to become more and more proud of her the longer they remained friends and colleagues. Carmen happened to be reading a book at the time in hopes of helping a student who had been diagnosed with ADHD. The book was called *The Motivation Breakthrough: 6 Secrets to Turning on the Tuned-Out*

Child and she found it just as valuable with the adults at the school as she did the students.

One of the most valuable points in the book is that people are motivated by different things and one must know what motivates a person in order to move them forward. Lavoie writes that students are motivated by one of six things:

1. Power
2. Prestige
3. Projects
4. People
5. Prizes
6. Praise

Carmen began her administrative career motivated by power and became motivated by people. Sally was motivated by praise. The superintendent was motivated by prestige. Once Carmen knew Sally's motivation, it was clear to her that giving her credit for this wonderful discovery of hers was crucial to her future as an aspiring leader. The team asked teachers what they were motivated by and took that information into account when praising and rewarding people for a job well done.

The student with ADHD was motivated by prizes and his teachers were able to make a behavior contract that focused on what he should be doing and prizes that he would earn for doing it. This was much more effective than the traditional contract focused on what not to do and punishments for violating the contract. Creating a behavior plan that was focused on his particular motivation preferences worked better than anything Carmen had tried before. This was not much different than figuring out what motivates an adult and using different strategies with each.

LEADERSHIP REFERENCE: *THE MOTIVATION BREAKTHROUGH*

The Motivation Breakthrough: 6 Secrets to Turning on the Tuned-Out Child, although aimed at students with attention deficit disorders, turns out to be a great resource for motivating anyone. Lavoie starts by pointing out that there is no such thing as an unmotivated human. Some humans are just not motivated to do what we want them to be doing. A student who refuses to come to school for weeks on end is not unmotivated. He is simply highly motivated to do whatever it is that he does when he is not at school.

Motivation also can change from day to day. Students, teachers, and others can appear highly motivated one day and very low on motivation the next.

Lavoie goes on to make similar points as Daniel Pink about how rewards and punishment do not work as we often hope that they will. They are either short term or simply repress behaviors until the external motivation is gone. He also makes the case that a person's basic needs must be met before they can be motivated to do anything other than meet their basic needs.

Much of the rest of the book is spent discussing the "6 P's to motivate students." Understanding each of these sources of motivation will help a leader to improve morale and increase productivity. Lavoie finally points out that several very powerful ways to give power in order to motivate are to give ownership, allow choices, and to get a formal commitment. Many people are so deprived of success that opportunities for them to be successful are the best motivator.

REFLECTION QUESTIONS

1. How do you give credit to others who contribute to the school's mission?
2. How could you figure out what motivates your teachers? How could you take that information into account to improve your school?
3. How could your teachers use *The Motivation Breakthrough* to better serve students?

Chapter 22

You Raise Me Up

A good leader leads the people from above them. A great leader leads the people from within them.

—M. D. Arnold

Sally forgot to introduce the next speaker and blushed brightly when she realized what she had done. But the next speaker, Mrs. Toms, knew that she was up next anyhow and jumped right up to the podium. Again, Carmen felt nervous when she saw Mrs. Toms carrying a bag up to the stage.

"Many of you know," Mrs. Toms began, "that one of the first things that Carmen did when we received the STEM grant from the state was to purchase a 3-D printer and a 3-D scanner. Her big mistake was putting me in charge of it." The room filled with the laughter of people who knew that Mrs. Toms is a big practical joker. "So, one day, the students and I convinced Carmen to come and stand in front of the 3-D scanner. She had only been at the school for about 6 months and I was convinced that she would do anything to win some points. She did. At the time, I had joined the bandwagon of those who thought that Carmen was using us as a stepping stone. So, I made this."

Mrs. Toms slowly lifted out of the bag with a devious smile on her face, a 3-D printed character with a gigantic head. She then shook the character and the head bounced around like one of the bobblehead characters given out at baseball games. The bobblehead was standing on a huge stone—a stepping stone. It had been painted in school colors and was not flattering to say the least.

"The students thought it was hilarious. The teachers that I showed it to thought that it was appropriate. But we both turned out to be wrong about Carmen. So, with my limited CAD skills, I spent almost my entire summer last year making a new character as a sort of apology. Here it is." Mrs. Toms pulled another character out of the bag. This one was different as was her smile as she took it out.

The 3-D print had Carmen standing with her hands over her head in a "V" shape with 5 smaller characters standing in her outstretched hands, each holding a star above their heads. It had been painted in gold and stood on a base that said, "Excellence: Every Classroom, Every Lesson, Every Day—Sally Moore" around the base.

Through emotional eyes, Mrs. Toms continued, "The event that really sold me on your dedication was an afternoon when I was doing parking lot duty. I had kindly asked a parent to move her car from the red zone and she flipped out on me. She was in my face screaming. A nearby teacher with her door open called you and you literally sprinted to my rescue. You immediately stepped between us as a physical barrier and I immediately felt safe. I had seen you trending towards emotionally supporting us on the leadership team, but now I could see that your support had no bounds, even risking your own safety. This one instance made me realize that every time I'm near you, I feel safe."

Mrs. Toms turned to Carmen while she held up the new 3-D printed character and said with a shaky voice, "This is for you, Carmen. You've raised us all up in your tenure here. Many of us have become administrators and several have even finished our doctorates because of you. This school looks nothing like it did before you came and whether you like it or not, much of the credit belongs in your hands."

"We all love you and we hope every day to become more like you." Mrs. Toms and Carmen looked at the statuette together, hugged, and whispered to each other. Sally then returned to the microphone and announced, "Next, we have former superintendent, Mike Young connecting via video conference from Boston."

LEADERSHIP REFERENCE

No leadership books were referenced in this chapter.

REFLECTION QUESTIONS

1. How do you support your teachers? How do they know that you care about them?
2. Have you created an atmosphere of safety at your school where teachers feel free to have crucial conversations with you and with each other?
3. A common mantra is that employees do not leave jobs, they leave managers. Does the turnover rate at your school suggest that teachers feel safe working there?

Chapter 23

The Shallow Pool

Motivation comes from working on things we care about. It also comes from working with people we care about.

—Sheryl Sandberg

While a man with graying hair and a bow tie scrambled to set up the laptop and projector, Carmen was remembering Mike Young, then assistant superintendent and her direct supervisor at the time. Mike was on the team that hired Carmen, and seemed to be one of her biggest supporters at the district throughout her initial rough start. Mike is now the superintendent of a small district in Massachusetts and they keep in touch occasionally. After some feedback and echo issues with the sound, Sally said, "OK Dr. Young, you're on."

Dr. Young fixed what little was left of his hair as a joke and said, "Good evening everyone, congratulations Carmen. As many of you know, I was on the committee that hired Carmen. As all of you probably know, this school either ate administrators alive or was a hitching post for a short stay before moving on."

"There was not much experience in the pool when we did the paper screening, so we were hoping for a diamond in the rough with an inexperienced administrator. We sat, unimpressed, through almost a dozen interviews before Dr. Esposito. Although she had no experience and clearly lacked confidence, there was something about her that made me take notice. I couldn't put my finger on it at the time, but later, it all made sense to me."

"Every fall, we were required to do walkthroughs with our principals. We hadn't figured out how to effectively evaluate administrators, so this seemed as good a way as any. A team of intimidating, well-dressed district office staff with serious faces would escort the principal around the campus and whisper to each other after each classroom. This was Carmen's second year and the turnover was so high that she had 17 new teachers on staff."

Carmen blurted out, "It was 18!" and Dr. Young corrected himself. "Yes, it was 18. As we walked through classrooms together, I realized what I had noticed in Carmen during those interviews, it was a deep level of empathy, a high emotional intelligence, and simply a genuine caring for those around her."

"It was evident in these walkthroughs when she knew the name of every single teacher, including the brand new teachers and had a conversation with each one of them about one of their children, their spouse, or a college course they were taking. She knew each person at her school and cared deeply for each and every one of them. She knew details about them and cared deeply about their answers to her questions."

"This is what makes a great principal, not curriculum, not test scores, and not balanced budgets or on-time school buses. Any manager can make those little things happen, but only a Level 5 leader can inspire followers to go above and beyond for kids. Carmen did exactly that and time and time again, she reinforced that something special that I saw in her during those interviews. She built relationships, cared about her employees and students, and demanded excellence in everyone around her including herself."

"I remember one year, I was invited to attend Carmen's back-to-school celebration, as she liked to call the first teacher meeting before school began. Most people did not consider the first meeting of the year a celebration. During a question and answer session, microphones were passed around and one was given to a new teacher. Carmen called out, 'OK, in the back in the purple shirt.' and immediately regretted it."

"I saw Carmen after the Q&A session apologizing to the new teacher for not knowing his name and inviting him to lunch that afternoon to get to know each other. Most other people wouldn't have been bothered by not knowing this person's name, but Carmen was crushed by the mistake and made sure to rectify it immediately. She searched high and low, asked everyone she came across where she could find this person. She was truly, deeply distraught about it. She never once made that mistake again."

"Carmen calls everyone in this room her 'best friend' and she means it. She loves those she works with and that makes all of the difference in the world. Carmen . . . your genuine care for everyone around you made your school a wonderful place to work and a spectacular experience for kids. We will miss you and we wish you the best in your retirement. OK, it's 11:30 p.m. my time, way past my bedtime, but we'll keep in touch now that you have so much free time. Congratulations, Carmen, we'll talk again soon."

LEADERSHIP REFERENCE

No leadership books were referenced in this chapter.

REFLECTION QUESTIONS

1. Research suggests that emotional intelligence (EQ) is more predictive of success than IQ. What do you do to support and develop the EQ of your teachers and aspiring leaders? What do your teachers do to support and develop the EQ of your students?
2. Which of the characteristics of a Level 5 leader are you working to develop? How would it look if you mastered this characteristic?
3. It has been said that everyone's favorite word is their own name. What strategies do you have to ensure that you know all of your employees' names and at least basic facts about them?

Chapter 24

The Matrix

If you want your team to achieve something bigger than you could achieve alone, if you want to "burst the bounds of your brain," you have to care about the people you are working with.

—Kim Scott

Dr. Vasquez returned to the microphone with agenda in hand. She spoke into the microphone, "At this point in the agenda, I am going to invite anyone who would like to come up to the stage and share with us the best advice that Dr. Esposito ever gave you." She turned to Carmen and jokingly added, "Maybe we should limit this to the period after your first 3 years as principal?"

A short line formed near the stairs to the stage. Carmen could not really see who was in line because she had been crying on and off for over an hour and she was avoiding eye contact so as not to start crying again. She thought that if she did not look up, maybe the entire situation would just go away. It did not go away.

The first voice came through the microphone, Carmen recognized it as a project director who she hired to write grants, do public outreach, and handle social media. He said, "I know that it sounds strange, Carmen, but the best thing that you ever said to me to make me a better employee is that you were under-whelmed with my work. I had learned bad habits at my previous school and that was the brutal honesty that you gave me that day."

"I truly needed to snap out of it and work hard for the cause again or I was going to tank my career. I cannot thank you enough for being so candid with me that day. I would not be where I am today if not for that comment." He began to walk away and quickly returned to the microphone, "I should add that not even a month later, we had a conversation where she shared with me how happy she was with my new work ethic and we got a $700,000 grant shortly thereafter. That's how we started our STEM summer school program. I didn't want to leave you thinking that she had been mean to me when she actually changed the trajectory of my career for the better."

The next voice was not as familiar, but became clear once the story began. "Dr. Esposito, you were the one who encouraged me to get my admin credential and I really wanted to develop my leadership skills under you, but the timing didn't work out. You never made me feel guilty about leaving for another school and even said how happy you were for me getting a vice principal position even though you were sad for the school that I was leaving. But the best advice that you ever gave me was in our exit meeting."

"You had just been through some difficult decisions and the school made the newspaper (not in a good way) several times that month. You told me, 'Live a life of undivided integrity. Before you make any decisions, think about how it would look on the front page of the newspaper.' I still think about that advice every single day and it has served me well. When all of the other schools were playing games with graduation rates, I decided to be honest with our numbers. Just as you predicted, they all ended up in the newspaper for it and my school did not."

Carmen felt so proud to hear these comments. To hear that advice that her father had given her was also helping someone else made her glow inside. Then to hear that one of her favorite books was having an effect on another was just the icing on the cake. She was feeling a little bit less uncomfortable now.

"Thank you for caring enough to give such wonderful advice to someone who was abandoning ship for the enemy. You taught me to be a great leader and your influence has reached outside the boundaries of your own school. I appreciate what you have done for me a great deal and I can never thank you enough."

The next speaker on stage had a distinctive voice. He was another member of a cohort of teachers who all worked on their admin credentials and became successful leaders along their own unique paths. This particular teacher took his leadership skills to the educational textbook industry and became a great regional sales manager.

He said, "As you know, Carmen, I am not a people person. I'd rather send 10,000 emails than make one phone call and I'd rather make 10,000 phone calls than have one face-to-face. I avoid conflict like it is a deadly, contagious disease. Once, when I was avoiding conflict and trying to figure out a lose/lose compromise that would help me avoid it, you gave me the best advice of my career, 'It is all about relationships.' You taught me to meet face-to-face, go to the social events, and ask good questions."

"As a pair of introverts the two of us, you taught me how to overcome my social anxiety and unfounded fears about face-to-face interactions. I would still be huddled in my office writing white papers that nobody will ever read if not for your advice, mentoring, and the great example that you set for me. You showed me that an introvert can still be a great leader. Thank you."

The next speaker walked up the stairs sheepishly with a stack of papers in her hand. She didn't make eye contact with Carmen as she approached the microphone. Her quivering voice came through and she said, "Carmen, I need to apologize to you. When you first started, we didn't think you would last so long. We had a history of bad administrators and terrible faculty meetings. So, we made up games to help pass the time. I am embarrassed that I participated in these games."

"One of the games was to keep a Google Doc with all of the verbal slip-ups that you made. It started out as a joke. But as we learned to appreciate you and your deep care and support for us, we stopped playing all of the games except this one. But it changed from a joke to an honor. We went from collecting these quotes to poke fun at you to collecting these quotes because we enjoyed your sense of humor. I now would like to read some of my favorite quotes from the list and pass an autographed copy along to you.

Top 3 Favorite Carmen-isms:

(3) I care, but I really don't care.
(2) Sure, you can sit by me, but not over here.
And our all-time favorite Carmen-ism
(1) Are you going to drive or am I NOT going to drive?

I hope you see that this was continued out of love and I hope that in your retirement, you can flip through that stack and laugh and reflect like I did as I was printing them. Thank you for always being a good sport and for always having our backs. You mean a great deal to all of us and we will keep this document of quotes to remind us of all of the good times we had together."

Dr. Vasquez returned to the microphone and said, "OK, enough of that! Carmen is squirming in her chair back here. I want to give Carmen one last opportunity for closing comments and then we'll end this ceremony and you'll have an opportunity to speak with her personally."

Carmen dragged herself to the microphone one last time in her nearly completed career. "I want to thank you all again. We are here celebrating me, but none of this was my doing, it was all yours. It has been a wonderful adventure and I appreciate you all. Before we end, I want to encourage you all to find your own Dr. Scaffale. Above my computer in my office, I had a small poster with my personal philosophy written on it. It was an assignment in one of my Ph.D. classes. I've included it on a card in your gift bags."

(1) Read everything that has been written about being better at your work.
(2) Do your work with pride every single time.
(3) Do more than you are asked to do.
(4) Be positive.
(5) Be empathetic.

Reading everything there is on leadership is my number one core belief and I hope that I've influenced you in that direction as well. There is one book that I wish I had read earlier in my career and all of you leaders and aspiring leaders would benefit from it as well. Every year in my evaluation, teachers would give me feedback that I am very nice, but sometimes I need to be more direct. I completely agreed, but I felt incapable."

"And then I read Radical Candor by Kimball Scott. The philosophy behind this book is to 'care personally and challenge directly.' On the inside, I totally believed in this philosophy and I wanted to be good at it, but it was a challenge for me. One of the things that finally convinced me was a story that the author told about having to fire an employee for something that could have been addressed with direct feedback long ago."

"As an example, the author gives a hypothetical, say someone walks out of the restroom and their fly is open. You don't know the person very well, so it might be embarrassing to tell them about it. But the alternative not to tell them is worse. Then they'll walk around with numerous people seeing them like this, causing even more embarrassment. Or they'll walk into a job interview or important meeting with their fly down, causing even greater embarrassment."

"The best solution is to just bite the bullet and tell them. Trying to avoid minor discomfort causes greater discomfort. It took me many years and I never perfected this, but once I did put it into practice to the best of my ability, I wished that I had started much sooner. Telling a project manager that I was under-whelmed with their performance was one attempt at Radical Candor early in my transformation."

"It probably wasn't the wisest choice of candid words, and it certainly didn't fit the situation/behavior/impact template that the author suggests. That comment may have bordered on the 'Obnoxious Aggression' end of the matrix. Considering that I started deep into the 'Ruinous Empathy' end of the matrix, at least I was moving." The crowd laughed hesitantly, beginning to feel that the ceremony, and Carmen's career, was coming to an end.

"I just want to say one last thing . . . again. It took me a long time, but I have now realized that there were a lot of great teachers at the school who were being held back by poor administration, much of it my poor administration. I want to deeply apologize for that. I was a micro-managing, teacher-blaming, inexperienced administrator. I believe that I have grown since then and all of you have as well."

"I spent the first half of my career trying to change people's minds with my words. Now, not only do I think that this is nearly fruitless, it may be impossible, and it certainly takes autonomy off the table. Just think, doctors give people choices like 'Stop smoking or you'll die' and 'Start exercising or you'll die' and people choose to continue smoking and not to exercise."

"So, how do leaders think that they are going to change someone's mind about collaboration, technology, or grading? Leaders can guide and influence teachers, but cannot change their minds per se. For incredibly resistant teachers or incredibly important decisions, an administrator can change a teacher's behavior, but that doesn't necessarily change their mind and should be saved as a last resort. Instead, I've found that a leader can change a person's actions, demonstrate results, and that . . . changes minds."

"I've found that facts and data don't change most people's minds. Many administrators before me used fear to try to change minds. I've read that fear is a good motivator to stop doing something, but not a motivator to do something and I completely agree. Besides, once the source of fear is gone, then so is the motivation. The two things that I have found that can change minds are hope and relationships. I hope every day that I have provided both of these things for you."

"A school is only as great as its teachers and this is an amazing school. You should all be proud of what you've accomplished and thank you for allowing me to come along for the ride. We realized together that the best way to ensure that all students are being served by the school is through the equity of great instruction. You are all excellent. You always have been, it simply took me some time to realize it. Thank you for your patience."

Dr. Vasquez jumped in now and cut her off before Carmen started telling more stories. She took the microphone and said, "Carmen has agreed to stick around for as long as it takes for everyone to get their hug, share a story, and say farewell. Before we do, however, let's end this the same way that Carmen ended every one of her faculty meetings with the chant." In unison, everyone chanted, "Excellence: Every Classroom, Every Lesson, Every Day."

LEADERSHIP REFERENCE: *RADICAL CANDOR*

Radical Candor: Be a Kick-Ass Boss without Losing Your Humanity is written by Kimball Scott who has been a leader at Google, Twitter, DropBox, Qualtrix, and others. Throughout her years of high pressure leadership, she has learned a great deal and developed her own philosophy of leadership that is based upon the foundation of Radical Candor. Radical Candor, in essence, means caring deeply for the people that you work with and deliberately and directly being honest with your feedback to them.

The author gives an example of Radical Candor when it was used on her by a leader. After a presentation, the supervisor explained to her that she said "umm" too much. She brushed it off and made a joke about it. The supervisor reiterated more strongly that she was serious and she should stop saying "umm" so much. Again, she made light of the suggestion and kept walking. Her supervisor then stopped walking, looked straight into her eyes and told her that she sounds dumb when she speaks that way and she needs to immediately get a speech coach. Kim got the message, got a speech coach, and never said "umm" again.

Ms. Scott explains a matrix with one axis being "care personally" and the other being "challenge directly." One who is high on both axes is practicing Radical Candor. One who is low on care and high on candor is considered obnoxiously aggressive. One who is high on care and low on candor (like Carmen early in her career) is considered ruinously empathetic. A leader who is low on both care and candor is considered manipulatively insincere. Kim Scott explains how to build enough trust on the team, invite debate, and make feedback a two-way street before Radical Candor can be effective. Considering that each of those factors is also good for teams and leaders, there is a synergistic effect when they all work together.

REFLECTION QUESTIONS

1. Who are you not being candid with and what harm is it causing? How do you fix this?
2. How do you provide hope for your teachers? How can you provide even more hope?
3. After reading Carmen's story, write down five vows that you intend to accomplish to ensure Excellence: Every Classroom, Every Lesson, Every Day on a card and refer to it daily.

Chapter 25

Epilogue and Discussion

Although this story is a work of fiction, most of the events are based upon actual events that I experienced throughout my career as a teacher, as I coached administrators and worked with leadership teams to improve schools or as a site administrator myself. I moved straight from the classroom to the county office without having been a site administrator but my job included coaching administrators who had been at the helm for twenty or more years. It was imperative that I read voraciously to be a valuable resource to these spectacular leaders. The books in this story are the ones that helped me the most in my work with underperforming schools with stories from my own leadership journey weaved in.

Some of the experiences were depressing and caused me to lose sleep. The math department meeting where only 3 percent of the students in the entire school were proficient was real. The response to the dearth of proficient math students, "That's just XXX High School students" was real also. The story about providing data to prove that spreading algebra over two years did not really work was real, too. This is a school whose only solution to their 3 percent math proficiency problem was 1 hour a week of voluntary tutoring in one classroom with twenty chairs.

When a faculty blames someone else for the school's shortcomings, why would the faculty ever read a book or attend a conference or take professional development seriously? Their explanations for the poor student performance were so illogical that it was unfathomable that an adult could have possibly believed them. There were data, historical trends, and classroom walkthrough anecdotes that contradicted these teachers' beliefs about students, but they believed them deeply anyhow.

This blame game was a huge hurdle and the only way to get over it together was to build relationships, to join their community of teachers, and then to move them out of their bad habits with collaboration, carefully selected data, and small victories. With less than a year of working with the school, the math proficiency rose to double digits even as the school was in personnel turmoil. Double digits does not sound like much to brag about, but the school went from 70 proficient students to 260 in less than one year. That's another 190 students who now have a chance of being successful in college and beyond and that was a great start.

One of my colleagues who was trained as a marriage and family therapist before becoming a teacher and then administrator told me many times that the way to help someone who cannot see the obvious truth is to "join them in their delusion." He used the movie *What about Bob* as an example. In the movie, a therapist joins a patient in his delusion and then they slowly take baby steps out together to bring him back to reality.

I never understood this until the 3 percent proficiency of math department. Against all of my best judgment, he encouraged me to pretend like I also believed that the students at this school were already achieving everything that they were capable of and then slowly, together, realizing that they are actually capable of much more.

To my surprise, it was a spectacular technique. We more than tripled math proficiency even though the economy was crashing and the school was about to be flipped upside down. The state was going through a new program for "persistently underperforming schools" and half of the teachers were transferred out of the school and new teachers brought in. The principal was also replaced as part of this turnaround program.

Yet, through all of this upheaval, in the most recent year of state testing (eight years later), the mathematics proficiency of this school is still more than 400 percent higher than it was when we started working together. One of the quotes that motivated me during these difficult transitions was, "It's about progress, not perfection." There were good teachers at this school who were being discouraged by jaded veteran teachers and chased away to other schools. Leadership was in a stalemate and morale was low. But using some of the techniques of the fictional Dr. Esposito, the faculty was able to make a complete turnaround. *Learning by Doing* and PLCs were a large part of the content of our work.

The REAL Committees were also real. Another colleague and friend that I worked with at the county office taught at a school that implemented REAL Committees before he retired and became a consultant. The results were amazing, so we considered implementing a similar program at a low-achieving continuation school that we were contracted with to boost achievement.

When we first began with this school, the principal told us, "If I could run away, I would." The first leadership meeting that we attended turned into a near physical brawl, fighting over trust issues and distribution of power. There was yelling, accusations, and even tears. This school was also identified as one of the "persistently underperforming schools" by the federal government, meaning that it was in the bottom 15 percent of all schools in measures of academic success for multiple years in a row.

Instead of choosing to remove half of the teachers like the previous school did, they chose to restructure the school completely and hired us as consultants to assist in the transformation. This continuation school had become a credit recovery, packet-completion school and sought to get back to classroom-based direct instruction as part of the transformation.

Motivation and trust were the big cultural issues at this school (there were also instructional issues). We worked with the school for many months on the typical school improvement agenda: collaboration, curriculum, interventions, and most of all, relationships. After working diligently on relationships and building the leadership capacity of the leadership team, we proposed the idea of the REAL Committees. The teachers liked the idea, but they thought that something was missing.

They felt that none of the committees directly addressed students, so this particular school made the idea their own by adding a "Student" committee and making them "REALS" Committees. Giving teachers decision-making ability and autonomy made all the difference in the world at this school. They already had some excellent teachers and teacher leaders, but they were being held back by the packet-based curriculum and ineffective teacher/leader relationships.

Through the implementation of these REALS Committees, the entire culture of the school changed for the better. Some veteran teachers worried that students would not be able to complete credits as fast as they used to, but acknowledged that the credits were being earned without much accompanying learning. The faculty really connected and began working together for the benefit of students. The principal ended up trusting her faculty and loving her job.

The school eventually won multiple awards and honors and even spoke about the REALS Committees at a national conference. The first year with the school, the state's goal for their Academic Performance Index (API) improvement was fifteen points. The school increased sixty points. That is unprecedented among California schools, particularly continuation schools. The school transformed from a packet-based credit recovery program to a school where powerful instruction took place and students still graduated on time. The REALS Committees had a great deal to do with that transformation. Repairing the teacher/administrator relationship had even more to do with the success.

After the transformation, teachers at this school were collaborating, going above and beyond what they were asked to do, designing new programs and interventions, involved in the hiring of new faculty like never before, participating in district meetings to create curriculum, inviting guest speakers, raising expectations, and increasing student supports. The turnaround was almost unbelievable.

One of the most important turnaround moments was when one of the teachers on the leadership team stood up and said, "We need to change the way we do things here. You guys hand-feed us materials to present verbatim to the staff at faculty meetings like you know the teachers better than we do. Let's try something new. Just teach us something and let us figure out how to present it to the faculty."

This was an incredible breakthrough and was a great leap forward. We role-played resistant teachers using *Practice Perfect* techniques, practiced engagement strategies, and sat back while the leadership team masterfully presented materials better than we would have ever done ourselves. These teachers who originally resisted meeting at all requested an additional meeting per month because they had so much valuable work to do.

Just as in Carmen's story, one of the ways to measure the effectiveness of leadership is how many leaders, both formal and informal, are inspired to take on leadership activities of their own. All of the leadership team and most of the teachers now felt like they were leaders at the school and that is a powerful motivating factor.

At least two of the teachers have moved on to formal leadership positions. They have invited us back several times to celebrate new victories with them and the growth and improvement just keeps on coming. The school is completely unrecognizable now. The principal moved on to a county office, the teachers are happy, and students are earning even more credits than they did when they were just completing packets.

Fortunately, the inter-richment story is also true. Although this is an absolutely wonderful program, the reason that I included it is because of the process leading up to the final iteration and how it demonstrates how incredible autonomy, mastery, and purpose can actually be. As science coordinator, I led a group of science teachers to visit a school that had an after school program that was achieving great results. Parents signed a contract at the beginning of the year that said that if students failed an exam covering essential standards, they could come after school for three days for reteaching to earn the right to retake the exam. The teachers collaboratively selected the essential standards, wrote the common assessments, and tested them for consistency and accuracy.

A group of teachers from another school that attended the visit decided that they liked the idea, but their students played sports, had jobs, and had family commitments after school so this schedule would not work for them. They decided to try Saturday school because many of the students who failed exams failed because they were absent and would be at Saturday school anyhow. This was a great idea, but still not the most important part of the story.

The important thing is that these teachers measured the success of the program and analyzed the data together. When they realized that it did not have the effect that they were looking for, they tried several modifications and studied each and every one thoroughly for effectiveness. They finally realized that Saturdays were not going to work because the students who needed the intervention the most were skipping Saturday school also.

The only way to make sure that the correct students attended, they realized, was to make the sessions mandatory and within the school day. Together, they designed a plan to add three days of inter-richment to the pacing guide after each essential standards test. Students would be split into two groups, those who were proficient on the test and those who were not. Those who were proficient would perform enrichment activities such as additional experiments, team projects, performance tasks, and other engaging learning activities. Non-proficient students would go to intervention for two days and then retake the test on the third day.

Again, this is a brilliant idea, but it was the development and implementation that were genius. The teachers who lead the interventions and enrichment activities were carefully selected. Before and after each intervention, data was collected and tracked. Different methods of intervention were tested and studied until they were finally happy with the results. In the end, what worked was to have some of the proficient students or Advanced Placement students work with small groups of non-proficient students on carefully designed activities.

This team of teachers produced spreadsheets with red, yellow, and green highlights for students who went up, down, or stayed the same after the intervention. Their independent, research-based, data-informed, and fluid implementation of this program is a model that won awards and eventually was one of the things that earned their department chair a promotion to an administrative leadership role at the district office.

I am not necessarily recommending that you do peer-led inter-richment during the school day with your students, but I am recommending that whatever you try, you study it with the fervor that they did to see whether it is as effective as you had hoped and whether modifications could make it even better. I am recommending that you give the teachers the autonomy and the support to try their own interventions. I am recommending that you give them enough time to go through enough iterations to master their experimental procedures. And I am recommending that you communicate a clear vision that will drive their work.

The story about the double hand claps and clock catchers was also based on a true story. One day at a visit to validate an AVID National Demonstration School, I noticed that in each of the first five classrooms that we visited, teachers were doing hand claps and other physical and verbal cues to introduce transitions, redirect attention, and reinforce learning. I asked our teacher tour guide, "Do all of the teachers do the hand claps?" She looked at me like I was crazy and said, "Everything that we do here, we do schoolwide" as if the idea that there was any other way to do something was foreign to her.

I came to learn that the strategies were called "Power Teaching" and as we walked around, I realized that they truly were used across the entire school, having a powerful effect. Schoolwide strategies had become the norm at this school, the culture. One of the teachers had calculated that these strategies saved her 4 minutes per day of getting students' attention. That adds up to approximately 720 minutes or 12 hours of additional instructional time per year.

One of the biggest complaints that I hear from administrators is that it is so difficult to get faculty on board with new programs and processes. This principal had clearly figured it out. I wish I had asked how that culture came to be, but I did not. I am not suggesting that your school should begin using Power Teaching strategies. What I'm encouraging is that when you find something that works at your school, do whatever it takes to ensure that it infiltrates all of your classrooms to the point that it would be silly to think otherwise and would be obvious to an external observer.

The story about teachers refusing to attend faculty meetings and the principal falling back on what the contract says is loosely based upon true stories. One thing that I learned quickly in my travels is that if a principal needs to use contract language to motivate teachers to do something, the principal has already lost. The principal has lost trust, respect, and ultimately has lost followers and can no longer truly be considered a leader.

I once consulted with a school whose teachers informed me at my very first meeting with them that if I was considering doing classroom walkthroughs, that I should know up front that their contract does not allow anyone, "not even people from the County Office" (said with a mocking tone) to enter their classrooms without permission. When the principal offered to find the language in the contract that was being misinterpreted, I convinced him not to. Instead, we went on a campaign to earn the teachers' trust and respect in order to be invited into their classrooms.

See, if we had gone the contract way, we would have won the battle. Clearly there was no language that said that we could not walkthrough classrooms. But, we would have lost the war and the walkthroughs would have accomplished nothing coming from people who they did not trust or respect. It took four of us two years to earn their trust. But in the end, we were acting out scenarios with the leadership team to prepare them for department meetings, discussing the effectiveness of lessons, and analyzing data that we collected during classroom walkthroughs.

It was slow work, but any person could walk on campus and see the gigantic cultural shift at the school that took place during those two years. The first time I was on campus, there was a fight in the restroom and a student pulled a fire alarm sending hundreds of students walking right off campus or jumping over fences during the chaos. By the end of our work together, attendance had increased, graduation rates had improved, test scores went up, behavioral referrals went down, and there were no longer hordes of students walking around pointlessly during class time. The greatest part is that six years later and even with a new principal, those improvements are still a reality.

InsideOut Coaching is also a real thing. In my time, I had probably been through five different trainings on "cognitive coaching" and other coaching methods. None of them clicked with me or were very useful out in the field until I tried InsideOut Coaching. There was either far too much to remember during a potentially heated conversation, too many acronyms to remember, or too many maps to carry around to use during a coaching conversation in the other programs.

But InsideOut Coaching (although very similar in structure to the others) was simple and made sense to me. The short description presented here will not be enough for you to implement effectively, so I would highly recommend that you find a workshop nearby. If it is like the training that I attended, it will be two days, two days that will change the way you work with your faculty. It is easy to implement, easy to remember, and highly effective.

The idea of building a school around autonomy, mastery, and purpose is also an idea closely rooted in my experience. I have helped charter schools write their initial charter applications based upon these fundamental motivating factors. I was hired in my current position to help this middle school expand into high school grades. We decided early that *Drive* would be a big part of the school's design.

This school has a very rigorous, Advanced Placement and dual enrollment curriculum, so we were losing sleep over the fact that we have no control over these courses or how motivational they are. So, we designed a course that all ninth graders would take called STEM Studio. The idea behind the course is that groups of students would have an entire year and the support of their teacher to work on a project of their own choosing that they are passionate about with bonus for projects that have a community service component to them.

Most students took to this assignment like no other assignment we had ever seen. One group designed homemade heart-healthy dog treats and then hosted a marathon where runners were invited to run with their dogs. They handed out bags of their dog treats at the end. Another group built a large, portable hydroponics display for the school. Students learned the software necessary to create learning video games.

Another group made an automated aeroponics system that used humidity sensors to trigger vaporizers to water the roots of strawberry plants. One student attempted to build a drone out of tongue depressors and hot glue. We still have video of its maiden "flight" where it tore itself apart and almost impaled the teacher. He learned a great deal and is now a YouTube superstar making invention videos and will be headed to MIT after his missionary work is done. Other students made smaller projects and posted step-by-step instructions on the school's Instructables site. These groups made things like useless machines, robots, and night lights that looked like thunderstorm clouds.

The department data presentations were also a true story. I worked with a school early in the PLC era that was really ahead of the game. When we did PLC trainings, we did them at this school and took participants on tours of their collaborative meetings. Collaborative groups selected their own goals for the year, identified what data they would collect to measure that goal, and decided how they would analyze the data to determine levels of success.

After a couple of years of mastering this procedure, they decided that each group would put together a presentation about what they had learned and how it affected their teaching. One member of the team stood at the poster (they got quite sophisticated over the years) while everyone else circulated the room reading and asking questions. There were many "aha" moments, lots of note-taking, and many successful experiments spread to other departments in subsequent years. This school was also the genesis of the story of mentioning the rival school in a positive manner during a presentation and destroying a trusting relationship in just one sentence. The school was the rival to this PLC school, I was the presenter, and I was never invited back again.

Dr. Sandee's story was a combination of characteristics of data experts that the county and district offices hired to explain test data to teachers mixed in with some of the mistakes that I made as a budding data and research fanatic myself. The message about confronting "brutal facts" too soon was a lesson that I learned after several miserable experiences early in my data coaching career.

Brutal facts are a terrible way to kick off a relationship. Brutal facts are only effective AFTER a relationship is built. I also learned that if you need an expert to explain data to someone, then the data is too complicated. I learned that it is far better to present the expert's data yourself in the form of a story.

For example, in one presentation to a group about college-going rates in our region, I started off with a PowerPoint slide with 100 students on a bus. Then I deleted one for each percentage point of students who dropped out in elementary and middle school. The next slide was missing the number who did not make it to the end of twelfth grade. The next slide lost the number who didn't meet the graduation requirements or pass the exit exam. The next slide removed the students who did not meet the state requirements to attend college. The next was reduced by the number who qualified but did not apply to college. The final slide removed those who were accepted to a college, but never showed up (a phenomenon called "Summer Melt").

The final slide had fewer than five students on it and most of them were female. This message was far more powerful than a simple college-going rate or a complicated presentation by one of our data experts. I received more requests for digital copies of that presentation than I ever have for my charts and graphs. It also showed that when we say that 32 percent of our graduating seniors qualify to go to college, that does not count the ones who dropped out before the end of senior year, which can be a sizable percentage in some districts.

The county office still uses this presentation as an example of how to present data with a story. I have also used the *Visible Learning* quiz at many schools to drive home the message of how powerful teachers are without having to say it directly. I did not originally discover how powerful this message was myself. A teacher pointed it out to me.

The idea that schools always think that they are the stepchild of the district is almost always true in my experience, too. It seems as if every school in a district thinks that all of the other schools get everything that they want. Then, the next day, I would go to visit one of those other schools and they think exactly the same thing. This misperception can be harmful and it would behoove an administrator to try to extinguish this kind of thinking before it prevents collaboration, trust, and sharing of best practices. It seems as if the us-against-them attitude of schools versus district offices is pretty pervasive and harmful as well.

Unfortunately, some of the sad anecdotes were true also. The story about the student telling me that the sound of an aluminum can opening meant that the beatings would start soon was true. In my career, I have only had to call Child Protective Services (CPS) a few times and that was one of them. CPS is not allowed to tell us what comes of their investigations, but I do know that the student graduated and went to community college.

My current leader was the inspiration for the story of Carmen fixing the clogged drains in a rain storm. Teachers came out one morning to find the executive director with his pant legs rolled up, no shoes on, and hand-clearing disgusting, mucky debris from the drains in our piazza. It went a long way toward earning trust and respect of everyone who witnessed it. So much of administration heroism goes unnoticed behind closed doors. A public display of servant leadership like this is rare and valuable.

But I have also seen in my career that one careless action can destroy trust and respect that took so long to build. I was invited to present to a faculty at an underperforming school and as I was waiting to deliver my portion of the presentation, the principal had an activity prepared. She asked teachers to take a 3 × 5 card and write down all of the barriers to student learning. There was a prize for who could write the most in 3 minutes. Then they shared out and made a group list.

The office manager then brought out a shredder and the principal said, "Everything that you wrote down are excuses and I want you to put them through the shredder and stop giving yourselves excuses for why students can't learn." People yelled out in disbelief, teachers walked out of the room, and someone knocked over the shredder. This principal, who had a pretty good relationship with her faculty, destroyed all of that in one faculty meeting activity. Trust and respect were gone and that activity was talked about for years even after the principal moved to another site. Trust is a fickle emotion. It can take years to build and one careless moment to destroy.

I don't want to leave you thinking that school turnaround is easy. It is difficult, tedious, insomnia-inducing, long-term, all day every day work. I once taught at a school that was struggling. We were on the federal list of persistently underperforming schools, more than 85 percent free and reduced price lunch, some gang infiltration, and all of the challenges that go along with the trauma that these students had experienced.

I was relatively young and filled with passion and I was experiencing a great deal of success connecting with and teaching students at this school. Proficiency increased over and over again in my science classes, well above school average. Students enjoyed my classes and the number of sections of these science classes was mushrooming. I have written two books about the work that I did in my science classes at this school.

One day, I was sitting at a faculty meeting listening to teachers complain about students and announcing their zip code expectations of students right there in front of all of their peers. I had enough and stood up and made a long, passionate speech about how these students are just as capable as any other students, that they deserve the best education that we could offer them, and that it was the adults at the school who could work as a team and make these goals come to fruition.

I finished my speech with, "We should turn this school into one that people would want to make a movie about!" You could hear crickets chirp after I finished. A single teacher stood up and I was excited that there was at least one person behind me. She replied, "I don't want any movie cameras in my classroom." I almost walked out of the door and left the teaching profession right then and there. I stayed another four years at this school for the kids. It turns out that the county science coordinator was at that meeting and she worked with me for the next four years to prepare me to be a great science coordinator to help impassion science teachers countywide.

All of these stories came out of either conversations with colleagues, experiences at schools, or books that I've read. These are the three things that I believe can make all of the difference for a school leader. The most valuable resource that I possessed at the county office was the experience of visiting hundreds of schools a year.

No matter what issue a school faced, I had visited a school that had already solved it. Some administrators have been at the same school and in the same district for decades or an entire career. Their ideas are limited and their toolbox is barren in comparison to those who have experienced a variety of schools. Administrators need to make a point of collaborating with other administrators far and wide and visiting as many schools as possible.

County and state offices are always looking for administrators to do visits for awards such as Distinguished Schools, Gold Ribbon, and Models of Excellence. Get yourself on one of these teams to see the best schools around. Every high school must be accredited and accreditation commissions are constantly looking for volunteers to go look deeply at schools and find what they are doing well and what they need to improve. These are incredibly rich sources of spectacular ideas.

One of the most rewarding activities that I took part in were "Administrator Network Meetings" where principals would get together and discuss their approaches to the issues of the day. Each of these meetings produced more usable ideas and conversations than 100 workshops or conferences put together. Many administrators now participate in this kind of networking through social media. Professional Learning Networks (PLNs) on Twitter allow administrators to connect with the best administrators, speakers, authors, and bloggers. I have learned a great deal from these PLNs and the twitter chats that they host. Either find a professional network or create one of your own to exchange promising practices.

Administrators also need to read constantly. There are hundreds of educational leadership blogs online by some of the best administrators and educational researchers in the country. This book is the culmination of my own blog entries. I found that there were many great business leadership books and not very many educational leadership books. I started blogging about applying the research on leadership in business to school leadership. One of the common themes of my blog is that leadership books are all pretty much the same, based upon the same research. So, pick up a couple of books that will engage you and you will surely have the research covered. The titles mentioned in this book are my favorites and have had the biggest effect on my leadership philosophy. If any of them sparked your interest, please get a copy and read it to get the whole story.

It took me several years and many mentors to realize that leadership is fundamentally about two things: relationships and influence. Since influence is mostly about relationships, this really means that leadership is almost completely dependent upon the relationships built between leaders and followers.

The job of a school administrator is incredibly important. It is not a job that can be done well without dedicating yourself to being the greatest at what you do. To accomplish that, the principles in this book and the books discussed herein will be invaluable. The main role of the administrator is to hire, train, inspire, and retain great teachers. Evidence that this role has been accomplished is when there is excellence in every classroom, every lesson, every day.

Acknowledgments

I have been incredibly lucky to have been surrounded by great colleagues and spectacular leaders in my career. Each one has had an impact on my leadership style and many of them have stories of that contribution to my leadership in this book. Because some are mentioned in the book under pseudonyms and I'd like to protect the privacy of the schools that I have worked with, I will not give their full names, but I would like to thank the following people who will know who they are.

- As a teacher, I'd like to thank: Diane, Leslee, Grant, Jay, Jackie, Chris, Carol, Steve, Cecilia, and Bob.
- As a county office administrator, I'd like to thank: Maureen, Ed, Dean, Mary, Ranjit, Stephanie, Chris, Kenn, Nancy, Mike, Miceal, Stan, Lynn, Jerry, Jane, Lanelle, Nita, Shirley, Paolina, Wanda, Dave, Tina, Linette, and Mark.
- As a site administrator, I'd like to thank: Paul, Alex, Frank, Christi, Karen, and Tracy.

From these leaders and colleagues, I've learned patience, determination, empathy, grit, understanding, communication, and more. In addition to people, I've learned a great deal from the authors of the books that are featured in the pages to come. Books and academic research are where I go for answers. But the list of leaders above have taught me that building relationships with those around me and communicating well are also keys to being a great leader.

I would like to give special acknowledgment to two individuals who have done so much for my career. Nancy Pavelsky for working so hard to prepare me to be a science coordinator and Stan Crippen for teaching me so much about relationships and integrity.

About the Author

Michael Horton graduated from Crawford High School in 1990 and earned a degree in physics from San Diego State University (SDSU) in 1993. He proceeded directly into the teacher credential program at SDSU. A year later, he started his first full-time, fully credentialed teaching job at twenty-one years old. Mr. Horton taught chemistry, physics, physical science, makerspace, and computer repair for twelve years.

While at a schoolwide Title-1 school, Michael began experimenting with and measuring the impact of different methods of hands-on, experiment-based homework. He has written two books (*Take Home Chemistry: 50 Low-Cost Activities to Extend Classroom Learning* and *Take Home Physics: 65 High-Impact, Low-Cost Labs*) about his experience with homework that contributed to an over tenfold increase in student proficiency on the state test while those same students' math results remained stagnant.

Michael earned his Administrative Services Credential with a dream of becoming the county science coordinator. He achieved his dream job at the Orange County Department of Education in 2006. After two and a half years, he transferred to the Riverside County Office of Education (RCOE) closer to home. At RCOE, much of the job of science coordinator also included working with underperforming schools to improve student achievement, fulfil contracts with school districts, and perform state-mandated school visits.

Michael went on to work with the AVID program at the county office and is now the assistant principal at the Western Center Academy (WCA) in Hemet, California. WCA is a sixth to twelfth grade charter school focused on STEM subjects and college and career readiness. In 2019, WCA was ranked seventy-seventh best high school in the nation by *U.S. News & World Report*. Michael is also currently a School Ambassador Fellow (SAF) with the United States Department of Education.

www.ingramcontent.com/pod-product-compliance
Lightning Source LLC
Chambersburg PA
CBHW030143240426
43672CB00005B/244